3Ch - 3rd ed

Dream and Thought in the Business Community,

1860–1900

By Edward Chase Kirkland

FRANK MUNSEY PROFESSOR OF HISTORY, BOWDOIN COLLEGE

Dream and Thought in the Business Community, 1860-1900

Cornell University Press

ITHACA, NEW YORK

0565716

To E.S.K.

Preface

IN LAUNCHING this tiny ship on the storm-tossed waters of the era of the "robber barons," I wish first to disclaim any intention of starting or joining a crusade for the rehabilitation of this group or of enrolling an entrant in the currently fashionable conservative *versus* liberal sweepstakes. As a result of puzzling over the problems of methodology raised by this study, I have not sought out one businessman as "the model," to use a vanishing phrase; the problem of proving him typical would be too prolonged. Instead I have sought to immerse myself in the available statements made by businessmen in books, magazine articles, private correspondence, and testimony before Congressional and other committees and in statements made by the press and periodicals directed toward the concerns of the business world—for example, the *Commercial and Financial Chronicle*. Purposely I have played down contemporary academic thought and the very large body of criticism of the business world, not because these sources are untrue or unimportant, but because they have already received extended treatment. I have not entirely refrained from entering this territory. "They know not England who only England know." But from the statements of businessmen themselves, I have sought through saturation to acquire a sense of the corporate thought of the business community. When such a consensus eluded me, I have tried to indicate dissents and divergencies. Doubtless those who read this book can provide other exceptions.

In all this my point of view, my motivation, is simple. I regard the rich and successful as part of the human race, and an influential part; hence I wanted to ascertain, through historical methods, what they thought or thought they thought. I do not employ "dream" in this enterprise as a subscription to any theory of sublimation, suppression, or rationalization. I mean by it thinking which is unorganized and unsystematic. Of course these statements by businessmen may be dismissed as a mass of hypocrisy, but to measure words by practice would have involved a five-foot shelf of volumes. It is simple—and more valid—to operate on the theory that businessmen, like other groups, generally meant what they said.

Whether acts measured up to theory is the province of a different kind of book from this.

It is a pleasure to acknowledge assistance from Bessie Pierce, Richard J. Storr, Walter Metzger, Larry Gara, Richard C. Overton, and Fritz Redlich. They have either let me copy material in their possession or aided me by suggestions. At the Massachusetts Historical Society, Stephen Riley and others have given me every facility, as at Harvard have Arthur H. Cole and Robert J. Haynes. Once again Dartmouth College, though I am an outsider, has let me build the resources of its library into my way of research and writing. Cornell University gave the spur to these essays by inviting me to deliver the Messenger Lectures in 1956, and the John Simon Guggenheim Foundation through the grant of a fellowship has enabled me to devote a year to the exploration on a wide scale of the policies of the business community. My wife, Ruth Babson Kirkland, has typed the whole manuscript and helped bring order out of illegibility.

Edward C. Kirkland

Thetford, Vermont
May 15, 1956

Contents

Dream and Thought in the Business Community,

1860–1900

I

Panic and Pain

EXCEPT in those instances when certain businessmen have sought publicly through the democratic channels of corporate organization to capture control of railroads and merchandising outlets, or have held cabinet positions in the Eisenhower administration, most Americans, it may safely be presumed, can hardly give the name of a single great contemporary business leader. Only habitual and careful readers of the New York *Times* or investors and employees in the great corporations themselves can identify the presidents of American Telephone and Telegraph, United States Steel, General Motors, Dupont, or the Pennsylvania Railroad. It was not always so. Since they are at least known by name to this generation, we may assume that almost any of their contemporaries could have identified John D. Rockefeller, J. P. Morgan, Cornelius Vanderbilt, Andrew Carnegie, Jim Fisk, Jay Gould, and connected each more or less precisely with certain enterprises or circumstances. Roughly these men were members of the business generation between the Civil War and the turn of the century. The appellation, "captains of Industry," which Carlyle coined, was often applied to them; others, with a somewhat less certain ascription of authorship, christened them the "robber barons." Doubtless the phrase originally carried a taint of disapprobation; now it is a sort of historical shorthand to identify a generation of businessmen; it does not necessarily involve any value judgment. Be that as it may, the fact that these individuals are remembered is probably less a tribute to our history teaching than to their importance.

An examination of the attitudes of this business generation toward certain, but not all, social, political, and economic issues faces the handicap of silence on the part of some business leaders and of the lack of systematic thought and expression on the part of others. This fact has sometimes been made to carry the implication that the business community was too barbaric to think about what it was doing or not literate enough to put it down on paper. This charge is ludicrous. The causes for silence, when silence existed, were complex. For reasons which can be left only to surmise, some business leaders made a policy of secrecy. One of Rockefeller's favorite aphorisms was "Silence is golden," and Leland Stanford, of the Southern Pacific and other great railroad enterprises and onetime governor of California, was so cautious that when a friend greeted him with, "How do you feel this morning, Governor?" the latter replied suspiciously, "Wouldn't you like to know?" [1] Others were reticent, no doubt, because of diffidence. Business affairs and activities were dirty, dusty, and personal and occupied a low priority in any absolute scheme of values. Ideas on religion and politics might be literary material; conceptions about making a living were not such stuff as books and articles were made of. At the other extreme, some business leaders were garrulous. It is one of the most engaging characteristics of Andrew Carnegie that he broke out from silence. When others were withdrawn, he was the author of an autobiography and of a systematic work on American institutions, *Triumphant Democracy*, "designedly written in as light a style as I am master of," [2] and of a flock of magazine articles collected in five volumes. Nor was he the only business contributor to the periodicals.

Whether businessmen held back their opinions or disclosed them copiously, generally business situations were the spur to their thought. It is enough to note in this connection that the decades between 1860 and 1900

[1] Quotations from I. M. Tarbell, *The History of the Standard Oil Company* (New York: Phillips & Co., 1904), I, 68; II, 127; and S. N. Behrman, "The Days of Duveen," *New Yorker*, XXVII (Nov. 9, 1951), 56.

[2] *Triumphant Democracy* (New York: Scribner, 1886), p. vii.

were ones of extraordinarily rapid and enduring change. A youth entering business at the age of fifteen in 1860 would have faced a world of industry which manufactured hardly a ton of steel and where kerosene from petroleum obtained from driven wells was a novelty of a year or so. If he survived to retire forty years later, he would have seen the United States the leading nation in the manufacture of steel by all methods—steel had displaced iron—and he would have realized beyond peradventure that the oil industry was one of the great economic mainstays of the country.[3] Change of this magnitude and rapidity penetrated every cranny of the industrial structure. In 1886 the *Commercial and Financial Chronicle*, giving tonnage statistics for the dressed beef trade, commented incidentally that this beef industry "is a growth of recent years," and in the middle of the next decade it marveled at the fact that in 1860 probably nine-tenths of all underclothes were made in the home rather than in the factory.[4] In terms of communications, the same youngster of 1860 would have seen a nation with 30,626 miles of railroad; no transcontinental line yet connected the Mississippi with the Pacific. Forty years later the railroad mileage of the nation was 258,784.[5] More significant than mere statistics was the fact that the railroad had shattered the protec-

[3] *Commercial and Financial Chronicle*, LVI (Feb. 11, 1893), 228–229, (April 1, 1893), 520–521.

[4] XLII (April 10, 1886), 448; LVIII (Jan. 27, 1894), 160.

[5] Bureau of the Census, *Historical Statistics of the United States, 1789–1945*, pp. 200, 202.

tions which distance had once given to local producers and merchants and had made the market a national one. For instance, it was not now enough for the crossroads storekeeper to know the conditions of the local crop and the credit standing of his customers; he had to know what Sears Roebuck and Marshall Field were doing.

However great the technological disturbances wrought by headlong and heedless inventors and technicians, they paled before the perplexities inherent in new methods of management. How could the old ways of direction and control be adjusted to businesses which were new or were larger than they had been before? Whereas at the end of the Civil War informed observers were commenting that the optimum size for a railroad, from the managerial point of view, was one with 100 miles and a capitalization of five or six million dollars,[6] twenty years later railroad corporations of over 1,000 miles apiece operated just less than half the mileage of the country.[7] These are inanimate matters. If not more complex, certainly more intractable were problems of labor and personnel. Whereas employers had once assembled small working forces for shops and mills, now they were compelled to organize armies for large undertakings. Between 1879 and 1899 the average labor force in the steel mills of the nation increased from 220 to 412, and

[6] E. C. Kirkland, *Men, Cities, and Transportation: A Study in New England History, 1820–1900* (Cambridge: Harvard University Press, 1948), II, 444.

[7] *Third Annual Report of the Statistics of Railways in the United States to the Interstate Commerce Commission for . . . 1890*, p. 21.

in the late eighties the number of employees on a single railroad could amount to 36,000.[8]

According to the conventional sneer, those who met these problems of change successfully were well rewarded for their pains. Merit aside, in the realm of wealth change was also the order of the day. In the eighteen hundred and eighties, businessmen and others were recalling their youthful years when "a man that had a farm worth $1500 or $2000 was considered 'A, No. I' " and when the "richest man in town was worth some $4,000 or $5,000" and "a village where, if a man had $50,000, he was supposed to be a magnate." [9] Yet a reporter who visited Carnegie in his study after the steel king had sold out, at the turn of the century, his holdings to the United States Steel Corporation, calculated with awe that the former "steel maker from smoky Pittsburg" received an income of $40,000 a day. While an increase in the number of millionaires in the United States from a handful right after the Civil War to 4,047 in 1892 had wide ramifications for society, it also raised in some cases baffling problems and difficulties for the recipients.[10]

Apart from these particularities of change, the whole

[8] *Fifth Annual Report of the Commissioner of Labor, 1889*, p. 15; W. L. Thorp, *The Integration of Industrial Operation*, [1920] *Census Monographs*, III, 61.

[9] *Report of the Committee* [on Education and Labor] *of the Senate upon the Relations between Labor and Capital, 1885*, II, 438; III, 622.

[10] Andrew Carnegie and others, *Personality in Business* (Vol. IX in *The Business Man's Library*; Chicago: The System Company, 1907), p. 31; Sidney Ratner, *New Light on the History of Great*

era between 1860 and 1900 shook the business structure
by a succession of tremblors. The first was the American
Civil War, a conflict up to that time without precedent
as to the number of men involved and wealth consumed.
After a brief interval of respite and recuperation, there
ensued a series of business panics and depressions. Two
of them, 1873 and 1893, join 1837 and 1929 as the worst
in American history; that of the mid-eighties, though
less calamitous, slowed and distorted the economy.
Willard L. Thorp, who has surveyed the history of
business cycles in terms of contemporary reaction to
them rather than in terms of later measurement, con-
cludes that fourteen of the twenty-five years between
1873 and 1897 were ones of "recession" or "depression." [11]

Such economic disasters were measured for the laborer in terms of wages or employment and for the
industrialist and merchant, along with the farmer, in
terms of prices. While the general price index fell, with
vacillations not necessary to trace here, from a high
of 129 in 1864 to a low of 71 in 1894 and to the same
figure in 1896, the wholesale price of pig iron declined
by nearly two-thirds and of refined petroleum by over
90 per cent.[12] Under bludgeoning such as this enter-
prisers stumbled and frequently fell. In such times of

American Fortunes: American Millionaires of 1892 and 1902 (New
York: Augustus M. Kelley, 1953), pp. xxiii–xxv.

[11] *Business Annals* (New York: National Bureau of Economic
Research, 1926), pp. 131–137.

[12] Bureau of the Census, *op. cit.*, pp. 231–232; Anne Bezanson
and others, *Wholesale Prices in Philadelphia, 1852–1896* (Philadelphia: University of Pennsylvania Press, 1954), pp. 162–163, 237.

economic whirlwind statistics of failures furnished by credit agencies made gloomy reading. From a low point between 60 and 70 in 1871, their index of business failure rose to a peak of somewhat over 150 in 1877; from another low point in the early eighties, the index doubled for the panic of that decade and did somewhat worse or better (depending upon the point of view) in the depression of the nineties. With the exception of only a few years throughout these panic years, firms were failing at the rate of 100 or worse to every 10,000 concerns.[13] What this meant in long-time terms of overall success and failure in business was not clear. But contemporary observers were prone to assert that 95 per cent of all capitalists, "men carrying on business," failed. Since successful business talent was a rarity, the bulk of capitalists were in just as "precarious a position as other classes in the community." [14]

It has been the fashion to speak and write of the business generation that met these bombardments as if it relished them and perhaps brought them on for its own purposes. The favorite words to apply to this business group have been "primitive," "strong," "confident," and "enthusiastic." Even those who disapprove of material achievement have focused so exclusively upon the good fortune rather than the failures of businessmen and have

[13] R. A. Foulke, "Peaks and Valleys in Wholesale Prices and Business Failures," in *Behind the Scenes of Business, Supplement, 1942–1949* (New York: Dun & Bradstreet, 1950), pp. 13, 26–27.

[14] *Nation*, XLIII (May 20, 1886), 419; XLVI (April 12, 1888), 293; LIX (Nov. 1, 1894), 320; E. L. Godkin, "Social Classes in the Republic," *Atlantic Monthly*, LXXVIII (Dec., 1896), 725.

been so dazzled by business achievements as to subscribe unwittingly to the cheerful gospel of success.[15] I do not believe that the titans of the generation, confronted by an era of rapid and disturbing changes and without precedents to govern them, were either as omniscient or omnipotent as the conventional interpretation suggests. In fact their own words expressed quite a different and more normal response to the situation. Looking back upon his forty years in the "hazardous" and "perilous" oil business, Rockefeller wondered

how we came through them. You know how often I had not an unbroken night's sleep, worrying about how it was all coming out. All the fortune I have made has not served to compensate for the anxiety of that period. Work by day and worry by night, week in and week out, month after month. If I had foreseen the future I doubt whether I would have had the courage to go on.

"Those were days of worry," his wife recalled.[16] And Andrew Carnegie's famous and oft-quoted decision to stop making money was not solely an acknowledgment of the evils of wealth, as it is commonly interpreted, but also the bewildered expression of a man suffocating under a tide of money.

Thirty-three and an income of $50,000 per annum! . . . Whatever I engage in I must push inordinately. . . . To

[15] V. L. Parrington, *The Beginnings of Critical Realism in America, 1860–1920* (New York: Harcourt, Brace, 1930), pp. 7–17 *passim.*

[16] Quoted in J. T. Flynn, *God's Gold: The Story of Rockefeller and His Times* (New York: Harcourt, Brace, 1932), p. 201.

continue much longer overwhelmed by business cares and with most of my thoughts wholly upon the way to make more money in the shortest time, must degrade me beyond hope of permanent recovery. I will resign business at thirty-five.[17]

Though businessmen of exceptionally bold and speculative temper may have welcomed the high winds and enjoyed steering their craft to fortune through the current hazards of storm and wave, the generation as a whole was more prone to seek security and reassurance than to welcome upheavals. Stability was its watchword.[18] There were various ways to diminish chance and uncertainty. One was to resort to seers and others with a gift for penetrating the unknown future. Even so case-hardened and self-reliant a business operator as Commodore Vanderbilt relied upon the practical side of spiritualism. While he seems to have been drawn to spiritualistic séances by the comforting assurance he was communicating with his mother and son, he also sought information from a Staten Island seeress as to the future course of the stock market. Once he invoked the shade of Jim Fisk for celestial advice in his operations.[19]

[17] B. J. Hendrick, *The Life of Andrew Carnegie* (Garden City: Doubleday, 1932), I, 146–147.

[18] *Report of the Committee* [on Education and Labor] *of the Senate . . . 1885*, III, 98.

[19] W. J. Lane, *Commodore Vanderbilt: An Epic of the Steam Age* (New York: Knopf, 1942), p. 310.

But from time out of mind Americans had sought guidance in their perplexities not from mediums, but from the Bible, from the folk wisdom that recapitulated it and, more rarely, from the pastors who expounded it. Americans had relied upon God's law, moral law, or natural law. When it came to God, His directions were most clearly revealed in business matters with geographical associations. From Portland, Maine, where promoters were sure that the "Great Architect of the Universe left open" for a favored railroad "a passage through the White Hills," [20] to Chicago, where the *Annual Report of the Board of Trade* held that a delay of improvements on the Hennepin and Illinois and Michigan canals "would be nothing less than a deliberate refusal of the beneficent provisions, which, in the topographical features of the country, the Creator holds out for our acceptance," [21] the note was the same. Natural resources, other than contour lines, were prone to arouse similar reflections. George S. Coe, president of the American Exchange Bank in New York and an innovator within the New York Clearing House, was sure "that the high estimation in which [silver and gold] are held is so manifestly instinctive, and their discovery in kind and in quantity so consistent with social and commercial progress, as clearly, to indicate an inherent pur-

[20] Kirkland, *op. cit.*, I, 480.
[21] *Twenty-seventh Annual Report of the Trade and Commerce of Chicago for the Year Ended December 31, 1884. Compiled for the Board of Trade*, pp. xxix–xxx.

pose of Divine ordination for a currency based on specie." [22] He who marked the sparrow's fall was also quite capable of pointing a path to the correct answer to more abstruse problems. An obscure businessman of Burlington, Iowa, straightening out his thoughts about political economy and protective tariffs, wrote that "Almighty God has given to each quarter of His Globe certain peculiar advantages, and He has given His Creatures knowledge and instinct which impels them to build great steamships and immense railways to facilitate the interchange of each section with another." [23] Such precision was not at all unusual. The Bible stories were not so much parables as patterns. James E. Caldwell, Tennessee banker and utilities magnate, was writing to Theodore N. Vail about the "undoing" of the New York, New Haven and Hartford Railroad: "In other words, they were experiencing the Scripture Lesson of the Tower of Babel, which seems often worked out in practical affairs, and quite literally so in the case of the New Haven Railroad." [24] Perhaps this railroad's afflictions were due to the misunderstandings and even flippancy of its officials as to how God worked. Wrote its President: "Of course you don't expect me to take a great deal of stock in the notion that God punishes by

[22] G. S. Coe, MS copy of an address entitled "Silver Question," to the English Club, Feb., 1886, Coe Papers, Harvard Business School Library (cited hereafter as H.B.S.).

[23] J. F. Tallant to Edward Atkinson, June 18, 1869, Atkinson Papers, Massachusetts Historical Society (cited hereafter as M.H.S.).

[24] *Recollections of a Life Time* (Nashville, Tenn.: Baird-Ward Press, 1923), p. 227.

providential visitation in this Life. . . . God governs the world, I think, by general, and not by special legislation." [25]

In the late nineteenth century, talk of this kind seemed a little "old-fashioned"; more frequent was the reference to the laws of trade or to natural law. These might, of course, be related to the divine at one remove. Clerical commentators were pointing out that God being the supreme lawmaker, "God's government [is] clearly revealed in the laws of trade." [26] But businessmen were inclined to mention natural law with a secular emphasis. Their tone derived in part from the increasing vogue of natural science and its triumph in technology, but even more from the developments of those sciences closest to man—psychology, sociology, and biology. In this connection the advent of Darwinism held out the promise that it might be possible to put man upon a scientific basis. As far as the business community is concerned, it is not clear how much it derived the natural laws of trade, about which it prated so much, from reading the *Evolution of Species by Natural Selection* or Herbert Spencer's attempts at Social Darwinism. Individual businessmen used the phrase "survival of the fittest," referred to themselves as "evolutionists," and, when Herbert Spencer visited the country in 1882, joined

[25] George Watrous to L. C. Alsop, Feb. 28, 1883, quoted in T. C. Cochran, *Railroad Leaders, 1845–1890: The Business Mind in Action* (Cambridge: Harvard University Press, 1953), p. 493.

[26] James Bascom, quoted in L. L. Bernard and Jesse Bernard, *Origins of American Sociology: The Social Science Movement in the United States* (New York: Crowell, 1943), p. 484.

other groups at Delmonico's to tender him a large, laudatory banquet.[27] But this did not necessarily imply an acquaintance or acceptance of a general philosophy. Indeed in 1874 the *Commercial and Financial Chronicle*, in its discussion of failures during the current depression, expressly repudiated Darwinism as explanation. It left "this fashionable philosophy . . . to spin its shining web and to apply its specious theories where it can." It went on to grant, however, that the philosophy would reinforce such old adages as "Experience keeps a dear school, but she teaches well." [28] In short Darwinism may have done no more for the business community than to furnish a new terminology for old ideas.

Nor is it measurably certain how much businessmen read the classical economists, Smith, Ricardo, Malthus, or Mill, or their American popularizers and expounders, textbook writers in the field of political economy, like Arthur Latham Perry, Francis Wayland, and John Bascom—to all and sundry of whom the increasing vogue of natural law and science in economics has been ascribed. Certainly the business community had no Karl Marx to dispel its confusions and anxieties by explaining what was happening and what was going to happen; on this score in a period of change, the proletariat was a privileged class. Nevertheless the more articulate of

[27] Richard Hofstadter, *Social Darwinism in American Thought, 1860–1915* (Philadelphia: University of Pennsylvania Press, 1945), pp. 31, 32, 34.

[28] XIX (Oct. 10, 1874), 361–362.

business leaders and of course their spokesmen showed
an acquaintance with the English classical school and
with contemporary English and Continental economic
thought. Charles Elliott Perkins, president of the Chicago, Burlington and Quincy, whose formal education
ceased short of college, had read and assimilated Smith,
Ricardo, and Malthus. Noting in a somewhat oblique
fashion in 1876 the centenary of Adam Smith's *Wealth
of Nations*, the *Commercial and Financial Chronicle*
regretted that his doctrines "are by no means so much
studied among us as they were a quarter century ago,"
but hailed Smith as one who "has given valuable aid to
those persons who are required by the emergencies of
life and the demands of business to investigate and to
act upon their forecast of the future monetary and commercial movements of the markets." [29] Though he
thought it presumptuous "for one who has had only
a practical business training," one Henry Wood compiled in 1887 a volume entitled *Natural Law in the
Business World*. Its indebtedness to Smith, Mill, and
others was obvious.[30]

Businessmen in their dilemmas were not content to
rely upon a political economy drawn from the past. A
large number joined hands with some reformers after
the Civil War in an active program to develop and re-
fine Social Science. One group was in Boston, and on the
roster of the American Social Science Association, a

[29] XX (June 17, 1876), 577–578.
[30] Boston: Lee and Shepard, 1887.

typical Bostonian society, one half the names had business connections.[31] The first issue of its *Journal* declared economy to be one of the four main concerns of the Association and then sounded a reassuring note that "Social Science is not Socialism," which dealt "with Society destructively, pulling down rather than building up," or "Radicalism." Social Science "is essentially conservative." [32] The lead article in this volume was by Henry Villard, secretary of the Association. Within seven years he was to start his climb to transportation overlordship of the Pacific Northwest, climaxed by his election to the presidency of the Northern Pacific in 1883. Somewhat earlier than in Boston, a group of New Yorkers founded the Society for the Advancement of Social Science. In 1865 two of the members launched the *Social Science Review*. The first number ascribed the necessity for this publication to the problems arising from the confused experience of the Civil War. "We should, at this period more especially, render ourselves familiar with the natural laws which govern mankind in its social state; and study well the manner of producing, distributing, and consuming wealth." [33] The editors commended their journal to "the commercial classes, bankers, underwriters, share holders, manufac-

[31] "Constitution, Officers, and Members of the American Social Science Association, 1877," *Proceedings of the Conference of Charities . . . at Saratoga, September, 1877* (Boston: A. Williams & Co., 1877), pp. 162–171.

[32] "Introductory Note," *Journal of Social Science: Containing the Transactions of the American Association*, I (1869), 1–3.

[33] Quoted in Bernard and Bernard, *op. cit.*, p. 465.

turers, merchants, jobbers, brokers and shippers [for] the every day operation of business." [34]

Another possible avenue of succor and guidance was statistics. Even before the Civil War, Americans had shown that "passion for statistics" which General Francis Amasa Walker, progressive economist, organizer of the inclusive Federal census of 1880, and president of Massachusetts Institute of Technology, thought a characteristic of the American temperament.[35] From the Civil War on, the business community called for new or reorganized agencies to provide statistics which were "practical" rather than "political"—the Federal censuses had been established to determine the basis of Federal representation and of taxation if need be—and statistics which should be promptly and continuously provided to private enterprises. As the Philadelphia Board of Trade informed a Senate committee, the country could not rely upon antiquated measures "with the acknowledged growing importance of correct and reliable census statistics as factors in considering all questions of business and social economy." [36] Edward Atkinson, treasurer or agent for a group of cotton mills and a pioneer in industrial insurance, put the need succinctly and san-

[34] Quoted in *ibid.*, p. 474.

[35] John Koren, ed., *The History of Statistics: Their Development and Progress in Many Countries* (New York: Macmillan, 1918), p. 670.

[36] Letter from the Secretary of the Interior transmitting a report of the Superintendent of the Census, together with a draft of a bill, in response to Senate resolution of February 16, 1891, in 52 Cong., 1 Sess., *Sen. Ex. Docs.*, No. 1 (s.n. 2892), p. 33.

guinely. Better and more inclusive statistics might disclose *"the natural history of industry."* [37]

Being bookish men, scholars are apt to search for literary sources for natural law: Darwin, Smith, Spencer, and others. Being practical and busy men, businessmen in all likelihood derived their notions of natural law from their own experience and observation. As Atkinson impatiently informed one of his correspondents:

Now the fact is I have read very little political economy. . . . In a multitude of books there is much unwisdom, especially in respect to economic questions. If students who have got a little grounding in some of the old masters like Adam Smith, Turgot, and a few others, *very few*, would then cut themselves off entirely from reading for one or two years and study facts and conditions, there would then be a good deal of hope that the blunders of pseudoscience would be cleared away. [38]

On another occasion Atkinson confessed of one of his investigations, "No one could have been more surprised than myself when these conclusions developed themselves from the facts of life. I have but little time for the reading of books." [39] Whether one proceeded by study or observation, there was no doubt in business minds that the evidence would not displace but reveal the natural laws which governed trade. In the vulgar par-

[37] *Ibid.*, p. 67.

[38] Letter to D. C. Kellogg, Nov. 15, 1887, Atkinson Papers, M.H.S.

[39] "How Can Wages Be Increased?" *Forum*, V (July, 1888), 489.

lance these were "business principles." The laws of trade or political economy were in reality "the laws of human nature," "human nature as it is, and not as it ought to be, or as we would like to see it." [40]

The canon of natural law could not possibly be either short or simple. Certain laws, nonetheless, emerged through sheer repetition as universal and fundamental. One was the law of supply and demand. The array of economic matters—wages, interest, finance, money (Gresham's law)—covered by this law was immense. As Charles D. McDuffie, agent of the manufacturing department of the Manchester Mills, announced in reply to an inquiry about the justice of the distribution of the product between employer and employee, "The question is one of supply and demand, which regulates the price of labor and gold and men and every commodity." [41] Permutations of the law of supply and demand also accounted for the panics of these decades, for the "law of ups and downs" in business. Charles Harding, a Cambridge woolen manufacturer, joined McDuffie in believing, "It is impossible to keep supply and demand even, or uniform. There will be times when there will be a glut and when there will be a scarcity." [42] Overproduction led to unemployment and depression. There were certain prerequisites for, or perhaps better, attend-

[40] E. L. Godkin, "Cooperation," *North American Review*, CVI (Jan., 1868), 174; E. L. Godkin, "The Prospects of the Political Art," *North American Review*, CX (April, 1870), 407–410.

[41] *Report of the Committee* [on Education and Labor] *of the Senate . . . 1885*, III, 67.

[42] *Ibid.*, III, 50, 290.

ant circumstances upon, the sound operation of the law of supply and demand. That law meant that the economy was organized on the competitive basis. The principle of competition is an economic law. This is "the law by which Providence secures the progress of the human race. . . . It is a law of human nature." [43] Godkin, editor of the *Nation*,—for I am quoting him—here goes on to assert that it was a law of liberty, for freedom was essential to the operation of it.

Finally, since the business community applauded Emerson's dictum: "Mankind is as lazy as it dares to be," [44] it believed incentives were required for economic activity. With the business world that incentive was profits. Joseph Medill of the Chicago *Tribune* tried to convince mechanics, his own directly and others through his paper, that a man "carrying on manufacturing . . . has behind his motive gain, and if he does not see a reasonable prospect of making a satisfactory profit on his investment, he will quit the business and not risk its dangers and losses." [45] Profit leads to property, by a development quite apparent. In its acquisition and enjoyment men must feel secure. Furthermore in the acquisition of property men will be unequally successful. "The great law which nature seems to have prescribed for the government of the world, and the only law of

[43] Godkin, "Cooperation," *op. cit.*, p. 173.
[44] Edward Atkinson, *The Industrial Progress of the Nation* (New York: Putnam, 1890), p. 11.
[45] *Report of the Committee* [on Education and Labor] *of the Senate . . . 1885*, II, 992.

human society which we are able to extract from history, is that the more intelligent and thoughtful of the race shall inherit the earth and have the best time, and that all others shall find life on the whole dull and unprofitable." [46] As the quotation implies, the benign operation of natural law in economics depended upon the possession of certain qualities: thrift, postponement of immediate enjoyment, industriousness, and "being frank and honest with oneself about one's affairs." [47] All this might be a myth; businessmen as well as clerics, editors, and hack writers expressed it.[48]

One advantage of secular interpretations of natural law was that these made it easier to divorce benevolence and other moralities from political economy. The inclusion of such elements raised complex, disturbing, and irrelevant problems. John D. Rockefeller demonstrated the operational advantages of separating morality and business. "These experiences with my father remind me," said the oil king,

that in the early days there was often much discussion as to what should be paid for the use of money. Many people protested that the rate of 10 per cent. was outrageous, and none but a wicked man would exact such a charge. I was accustomed to argue that money was worth what it would

[46] E. L. Godkin, "Duty of Educated Men in a Democracy," *Forum*, XVII (March, 1894), 43.

[47] J. D. Rockefeller, *Random Reminiscences of Men and Events* (New York: Doubleday, 1933), pp. 74–76.

[48] I. G. Wyllie, *The Self-Made Man in America: The Myth of Rags to Riches* (New Brunswick, N.J.: Rutgers University Press, 1954), *passim*.

bring—no one would pay 10 per cent., or 5 per cent., or 3 per cent. unless the borrower believed that at this rate it was profitable to employ it. . . . All the arguments in the world did not change the rate, and it came down only when the supply of money grew more plentiful.[49]

This statement implies also another general characteristic of the laws of trade or laws of political economy. They were inevitable and immutable, for the characteristics of human nature were everywhere and always the same.[50] It would be endlessly diverting, in one sense, to assemble a garland of the figures of speech used to drive home this point. Again and again the area of natural science, physics, chemistry, meteorology, and biology, and of common-sense observation supplied analogues for economic phenomena. Panics and prosperity were extremes of the "swing of the pendulum"; panics, "financial hurricanes," never occur "except as a growth from seeds which have long been germinating," and business changes were the alternations of disease and health. When disease lopped off weak members, like some forms of "organic life our economic system, quickly puts forth newer and stronger members to take their place." Joseph Medill announced, "that under the fixed laws of trade, of supply and demand, the employer

[49] J. D. Rockefeller, *Random Reminiscences of Men and Events* (copyright, 1909 by Doubleday, Page & Company; copyright, 1937 by John D. Rockefeller), pp. 47, 48. Reprinted by permission.

[50] C. E. Perkins, Memo, Feb. 6, 1905, Perkins Private Letters and Memos, Richard C. Overton (cited hereafter as R.C.O.); Rockefeller, *op. cit.*, pp. 71–75.

has really little more control over prices . . . than over the winds and the weather." [51]

The operation of natural laws was usually beneficent and always just. Charles Elliott Perkins, taking the idea of "social justice" to task for assuming that the products of industry were unjustly distributed, declared:

They are not equally distributed but it does not follow they are unjustly distributed. Is the rainfall unjustly distributed when an honest farmer loses his crop by drouth? Is the law of gravitation unjust when a child accidentally falls out of a second-story window and is injured for life? . . . If a man by hard work and intelligence, honestly acquires property and takes care of it, while his neighbor, equally honest and intelligent, acquires property and fails to take care of it, are the products of the industry of both of them unjustly distributed? [52]

Laws of such value had better be left alone. Nettled by Henry Demarest Lloyd's famous article on the Standard Oil in the *Atlantic Monthly*, Perkins wrote Atkinson,

The donkeys who can't see the operation of natural laws in fixing rates of transportation now rely mainly on the Standard Oil Company as an example. . . . I think it would answer an extremely useful purpose if as able a pen as yours would show what I suppose to be the fact, that the Stand-

[51] *Report of the Committee* [on Education and Labor] *of the Senate . . . 1885*, II, 992; *Commercial and Financial Chronicle*, XVII (Oct. 11, 1873), 479, (Nov. 29, 1873), 710; XVIII (May 23, 1874), 515; XIX (Sept. 26, 1874), 305, (Oct. 24, 1874), 410.

[52] Letter to the *Hawk-Eye*, May 21, 1894, Perkins Private Letters and Memos, R.C.O.

ard Oil Company is simply a product of natural laws and laws which it is not safe to touch. . . . I have *no* knowledge touching the Standard Oil Co. more than what I read in the newspapers.[53]

The statement reveals the ubiquity of natural law as well as the ease of reasoning from fixed premises.

In all fairness, it should be added that businessmen themselves sometimes entertained dissenting opinions from the view that a knowledge of economic law was of much immediate use. Even Edward Atkinson, who had calculations for everything, informed the United States Monetary Commission: "You appear to think that every business man enters upon a computation of statistical figures on every transaction; he does no such thing; he is guided by observations and does not stop to make statistics in regard to every transaction; if he did he would be apt to fail." [54] But this glimpse of actuality does not necessarily endanger the structure here set forth so much as reflect upon the imperfections of some of its details. When outsiders called in question fundamentals, the response of business spokesmen showed how firm a foundation the old faith enjoyed. Though the *Commercial and Financial Chronicle* might at first salute the "historic method" of economics as a desirable check on the utopianism and abstraction of political econ-

[53] June 7, 1881, Atkinson Papers, M.H.S.
[54] Report of the United States [Silver Commission] Monetary Commission, 44 Cong., 2 Sess., *Sen. Report*, No. 703, Pt. 2 (s.n. 1739), p. 278.

omy,[55] E. L. Godkin eventually discerned that the historical school was also the "emotional school"; that it did not so much provide laws as emphasize ethical ends to be served by the economy; that it was "simply saying to the rich what the 'Society for the Abolition of Poverty' says—that they are cruel or unjust."[56]

As this riposte and counterriposte suggests, there was an alternative explanation for the reliance of the business community upon the doctrine of natural law. John Roach, the shipbuilder, hinted at the other reason in 1885: "There are few persons who know the excitement and the fear that exists among capitalists today," and as imperturbable an operator as Jay Gould confessed "capital is scary."[57] About the mid-eighties the theme of natural law, for the vogue of which attempts at self-consolation and at the explanation of perplexing phenomena had once been chiefly responsible, was erected into a defense of business against attack. Who were the attackers? When Atkinson testified before a Senate Committee on Education and Labor in the mid-eighties, he identified one phalanx; in a prelude to his statement he observed that he appeared before the Committee at their request and not as a "voluntary philan-

[55] Joseph Dorfman, *The Economic Mind in American Civilization, 1865–1918* (New York: Viking, 1949), p. 88; *Commercial and Financial Chronicle*, XXI (July 24, 1875), 74–75.

[56] "The Economic Man," *North American Review*, CLIII (Oct., 1891), 492–500.

[57] *Report of the Committee* [on Education and Labor] *of the Senate . . . 1885*, I, 1013, 1089.

thropist." "I merely compile statistics, ascertain facts, and attempt to see what they mean," he later added.[58] To the "philanthropists" Charles Elliott Perkins, stung into epithets by current cant, later added "Professors and Lady Millionaires." [59] Under the rubric of "philanthropists, Professors and Lady Millionaires," could be grouped such "altruists" as Henry Demarest Lloyd and the Social Gospellers; the "altruist" is interested "in everybody else's business, he calls it loving his neighbor better than himself," sneered Perkins.[60]

But the new usefulness for a handy argument did not replace the old. Only our habit of writing the history of the era in terms of politics, Supreme Court decisions, and briefs of learned counsel has led historians to interpret the structure of business thought primarily as defense propaganda rather than as explanation or comfort for business insecurity in face of the "facts of life." Panic and perplexity, not pain, gave the first occasion for this sort of business thought.

The prevalent economic uncertainty also challenged the business community to bring disorder under control, to substitute order and calculation for confusion, to "rationalize," as we now say, the conduct of business. The visible implementation of these purposes was in this era the growth of big business and the consolidation

[58] *Ibid.*, III, 342, 344.

[59] "Scientific Charity: A Colloquy overheard by a *Hawk-Eye* Reporter," 1895(?), R.C.O.

[60] Memo, Sept. 29, 1902, Perkins Private Letters and Memos, R.C.O.

movement. That this accomplishment revealed flaws in doctrines widely accepted by the business community is clear, at least in retrospect. Obviously there was an awkward contradiction between the belief in competition and the fact of consolidation, between natural laws which men could no more direct than "they could make water run up hill" and the willed alterations in business organization brought about by trust and holding company, between law as immutable and law as growth and evolution. The few who were contemporaneously conscious of the paradoxes raised by business development sought to reconcile them. One explanation was to deny that the new tendencies were of universal application. The law of competition still applied to most business enterprises; [61] it could be modified but not stopped. Others met the situation by a higher synthesis. With immense patience and repetition, Charles Francis Adams, Jr., railroad commissioner of Massachusetts and later president of the Union Pacific, found that the law of concentration and aggregation of capital had a hallowed and remote origin—at least in the railroad world. George Stephenson, the father of the steam locomotive, had early uttered the aphorism, "Where combination was possible, competition was impossible." [62] But so little was rationalization able to tear itself free from old contexts that the natural law of competition simply gave place to that monstrosity, "a natural monopoly." Proba-

[61] Cochran, *op. cit.*, pp. 138–139.
[62] C. F. Adams, Jr., "Railroad Inflation," *North American Review*, CVIII (Jan., 1869), 150.

bly such contradictions and developments convinced few businessmen of the fallibility of natural law; that they weakened the case as a defense of the business system is certain.

II

The Big House

EARLY in the seventies, the railroad captains who had built the Central Pacific and had given California a railroad network in the Southern Pacific Railroad began the transformation of Nob Hill in San Francisco. On its abrupt, raw heights, Mark Hopkins, Charles Crocker, and Leland Stanford erected their grandiose palaces of brick and wood. Some of these buildings relied upon sheer mass for magnificence; others were equipped with towers, battlements, and other accoutrements of castles. Crocker's house, said to have cost $1,250,000, had a seventy-six-foot observation tower up which the corpulent host hoisted his immense bulk to point out to his guests the view of the harbor. Contemporary critics appraised these architectural achievements variously. One thought they brought "a bit of ancient Carcassonne to the shores of the Pacific"; another characterized Crocker's home "as a delirium of the wood carver" and asserted the common feature of the whole architectural array was an expense which could not be taken away from it.[1]

Almost at the same time, the great capitalists of Chicago were building more stately mansions. Though the Great Fire of 1871 perhaps made this decision mandatory, the first steps had been taken earlier. Marshall Field had purchased two lots on Prairie Avenue, the most exclusive street in the city. Commissioning the fashionable architect of the East, Richard Morris Hunt, to draw the designs, Field built a three-story stone and brick edifice topped with a mansard roof. Near at hand were houses in the Hudson River Gothic and French chateau style.[2] It was in the next decade that Potter Palmer, Chicago merchant, almost ruined by the fire and the panic, boldly rebuilt his fortunes and in the course of the process shrewdly eyed a marsh and city dump north of the Michigan River. This he bought, filled in with sand, and when the city ran Lake Shore Drive through it, built his own turreted castle of gray

[1] Oscar Lewis, *The Big Four: The Story of Huntington, Stanford, Hopkins, and Crocker, and of the Building of the Central Pacific* (New York: Knopf, 1938), pp. 68, 111–112, 134–138, 168–169.

[2] John Drury, *Old Chicago Houses* (Chicago: University of Chicago Press, 1941), pp. 35–37.

and brown stone with a tower and plenty of huge windows. In a sense this new mansion on the Chicago Gold Coast became a sort of capitol building for a city that otherwise had none.[3] It was "a mansion to end all mansions." It was "an American architect's best thought of what a baronial castle should be." [4]

In cities more settled than these flamboyant communities, the big house reared its bulk. In the seventies the brownstone uniformity and drabness of New York —a town "of narrow houses so lacking in external dignity," of which Edith Wharton complained [5]—began to give way, as families of wealth built the palaces along Fifth Avenue opposite Central Park or just below it. To be sure, the edifice which William H. Vanderbilt built in 1879 on the avenue between 51st and 52nd Streets was of brownstone rather than of red and black marble. Vanderbilt feared sudden death and brownstone was easier and quicker to work. The house was really three palaces in one and occupied an entire block. A sort of poet laureate hailed it: "Like a more perfect Pompeii, the work will be the vision and image of a typical American residence, seized at the moment when the nation begins to have a taste of its own." [6] A few years later, one

[3] Ernest Poole, *Giants Gone, Men Who Made Chicago* (New York: McGraw, 1943), pp. 105–110.

[4] Drury, *op. cit.*, pp. 128–131.

[5] Edith Wharton, *Backward Glance* (New York: Appleton-Century, 1934), pp. 2, 54–55.

[6] Wayne Andrews, *The Vanderbilt Legend: The Story of the Vanderbilt Family, 1794–1940* (New York: Harcourt, Brace, 1941), p. 221.

of Vanderbilt's sons commissioned Richard M. Hunt to build a chateau on the Avenue. Of limestone, it was a compound copy of the Castle of Blois and of a house at Bourges. Like his father's edifice, it was reported to have cost $3,000,000.[7]

But the rich were not content to be urban dwellers. Like other mortals they had to vacation, or perhaps live, in the country. They did not succeed, even if they had wished, in leaving behind the architecture associated with them. In Newport, a watering place conveniently near New York by the overnight Fall River boats, they converted a colonial town into the most spectacular of resorts. Along Bellevue Avenue and Ocean Drive the post-Civil War era tossed up a froth of castles. The Vanderbilts' were heavy with marble.[8] Designated "cottages" after the original seaside houses, Henry James thought these newcomers were better called "white elephants." [9] But it was not necessary to have an elaborate edifice near others. At Asheville, North Carolina, George Washington Vanderbilt, II, materialized in the mid-nineties a complete estate, Biltmore. The building, set in a forest and park, had a frontage, with stables, of nearly a fifth of a mile, forty master bedrooms, and a dining room with three huge fireplaces abreast at one end. This chateau, like other Vanderbilt

---

[7] *Ibid.*, pp. 251–252.

[8] *Ibid.*, pp. 267–268; Cleveland Amory, *The Last Resorts* (New York: Harper, 1948), pp. 170–172.

[9] *The American Scene, Together with Three Essays from "Portraits of Places"* (New York: Scribner, 1946), pp. 224–225.

ones, had Hunt as its architect. A labor force was imported from France to work the stone authentically.[10]

Why did they do it? Why did the business leaders from San Francisco to Bar Harbor have to live in houses with libraries, billiard rooms, art galleries, several rooms in which to eat, at least one of which had to be two stories high and paneled to the ceiling, buildings sometimes equipped with small theatres and perhaps even a chapel capable of holding a considerable congregation? There is an assumption here made by most critics that the owners of the houses conceived of them and wanted them. The antibusiness critics found this an acceptable explanation, and so did the architects who were prone to assume a wearied and frustrated air after their bouts with the tastes and budgets of their patrons. But the architects themselves may have been largely responsible for the extravagance of these edifices. An art dealer, like Duveen, sharpened the appetites of millionaires for fine art as well as instructed their tastes.[11] Architects, rewarded by percentage commissions, and the larger the cost the higher the commission, performed the same function when it came to housing millionaires.[12]

The conventional explanation for the big house has

[10] Andrews, *op. cit.*, pp. 331–335.

[11] S. N. Behrman, *Duveen* (New York: Random House, 1952), *passim*.

[12] Wayne Andrews, *Architecture, Ambition, and Americans: A History of American Architecture, from the Beginning to the Present, Telling the Story of the Outstanding Buildings, the Men Who Designed Them and the People for Whom They Were Built* (New York: Harper, 1955), pp. 194–197.

been that the robber baron, like his prototype abroad, demanded in his housing: bulk, space, and permanence.[13] This hankering was almost a matter of the genes. This biological link between wealth and houses has been analyzed with somewhat more acumen as well as persuasiveness by Thorstein Veblen in his *Theory of the Leisure Class*. Though he does not bear down upon housing in that essay, Veblen advances as explanation for architectural extravagance that in a pecuniary culture the leisure class, for example the businessman, demonstrated its honorific position by conspicuous leisure. As the opportunities for display through this channel shrink, the group resorts increasingly to conspicuous and unnecessary consumption. Big houses, like wasteful food and drink and sport and a classical education, are in this category.[14] Certainly the conception of the big house as a sort of visible bank balance fits in neatly with many contemporary developments, and accords with the persistent tendency to exaggerate the cost of the millionaire's mansion. Thus Marshall Field's house in Chicago was "said to have cost two million dollars"; [15] the actual cost of house, furniture, stables, and horses was, according to a memorandum in the Field papers, about $175,000.[16] If the purpose was display, imprecision of this sort is a positive advantage.

Like many generalizations, Veblen's was too simple.

[13] Miriam Beard, *A History of the Business Man* (New York: Macmillan, 1938), pp. 683–684.

[14] *The Theory of the Leisure Class: An Economic Study of Institutions* (New York: Macmillan, 1908), *passim.*

[15] Drury, *op. cit.,* p. 36.

[16] B. L. Pierce, "History of Chicago," III (MS vol.), pp. 50–51.

The motives for the big house were complex. Sometimes wives drove husbands to these expenditures; sometimes husbands undertook them as a gesture of romance to their wives. The newly rich who once, like as not, had lived in cramped quarters and as children slept several to a room, if not a bed, were now willing to pay handsomely for space and privacy. Nor was the chance to invest in a sound property or convert a poor one into a paying proposition lacking, as Potter Palmer and Mark Hopkins and others demonstrated.[17] However impelling such motivations for action, they were hardly usable as a rationale for the big house. Since all expenditure employed labor, the construction and maintenance of the big house made work; this was commendable. Thus Edward Atkinson in 1886 informed a group of Providence workingmen that Mr. Vanderbilt

built a most expensive dwelling-house, of which he occupied a part, his servants obtaining their shelter in the other part. . . . Such a dwelling is not capital. That is to say, it produces nothing. . . . It may be very foolish for the owner of capital, or of that which might become capital, . . . to spend it on fancy farms, palatial dwellings, or things of that sort; but in such expenditure he gives employment for that period during which the expenditure is being made to a very large number of persons.

The big house distributes money:

although it may not be the wisest method, it is the only method consistent with the present standard of education and opportunity. . . . I do not myself justify many of

[17] See above notes 1 and 3; B. J. Hendrick, *The Life of Andrew Carnegie* (New York: Doubleday, 1932), II, 259.

these lavish expenditures. I think that a man, however rich he may be, is very foolish to build a dwelling-house, which must be sold either by his children or his grandchildren, for the reason that none of them can afford to live in it under the righteous method of distributing property, which prevails in this country.[18]

Whether satirizing the Boston calculator or not, Mr. Dooley was cautioning his Hennessy:

Now, don't go gettin' cross about th' rich, Hinnissy. Put up that dinnymite. Don't excite ye'ersilf about us folks in Newport. It's always been th' same way, Father Kelly tells me. Says he: "If a man is wise, he gets rich an' if he gets rich, he gets foolish, or his wife does. That's what keeps the money movin' around. What comes in at th' ticker goes out at the wine agent. F'river an' iver people have been growin' rich, goin' down to some kind iv a Newport, makin' monkeys iv thimsilves an' goin' back to the jungle. . . . An' . . . I'm glad there is a Newport," he says. "It's th' exhaust pipe," he says. "Without it we might blow up," he says. "It's th' hole in th' top iv th' kettle," he says. "I wish it was bigger." [19]

A genuine Protestant minister, rather than a supposititious Catholic priest, preached the same doctrine. William H. P. Faunce, onetime Rockefeller's pastor and later president of Brown University, declared in 1893:

[18] "Address to the Workingmen in Providence, R.I., April 11, 1886," *Addresses upon the Labor Question* (Boston: Rand, Avery, 1886), pp. 22–24.

[19] F. P. Dunne, *Observations by Mr. Dooley* (New York and London: Harper, 1906), pp. 201–202. Quotation reprinted by permission of the publisher.

"The man who possesses a fortune is *nolens volens* a benefactor to the community. He may be a misanthrope and atheist. But if such a man moves into a western city and begins to spend his money in the most selfish and ostentatious luxury, he is an involuntary benefactor of that city." [20] In addition to employing labor the expenditures of rich men went for the support of art; wealth had been historically the latter's patron. Ornamentation and decoration were possible in a chateau, impossible in a cottage. The big house adorned and beautified the community. It was a matter of civic pride.[21] This was another justification for the private palace.

Defenses from expediency were probably more persuasive than the argument from right. Henry George made it clear that in his philosophy the rich man with money could do as he wanted with it. "If he gets his wealth without robbing anybody else, without preventing anybody else from having *his* fair opportunity to produce wealth, we can safely leave it to him and let him put up a pyramid with it, or make a big bonfire of it, or throw it into the sea, if he desires." [22] Indeed, some

[20] Quoted in H. F. May, *Protestant Churches and Industrial America* (New York: Harper, 1949), p. 192.

[21] *Twenty-sixth Annual Report of the Trade and Commerce of Chicago, for the Year Ended December 31, 1883. Compiled for the Board of Trade*, pp. 10–11; H. C. Potter, "The Gospel of Wealth," *North American Review*, CLII (May, 1891), 516; Andrew Carnegie, "Wealth," *North American Review*, CXLVIII (June, 1889), 42.

[22] *Report of the Committee* [on Education and Labor] *of the Senate upon the Relations between Labor and Capital, 1885*, I, 514.

commentators held that the failure of the capitalist to build a big house was an indictment of selfishness and greed. It was an obligation of the rich to live lavishly. Ida M. Tarbell, in a *McClure's Magazine* article in 1905, discharged against John D. Rockefeller all the buckshot she had not been able to use in her *History of the Standard Oil Company*. One of her accusations was the unpretentiousness of Rockefeller's homes.

No one of the three houses he occupies has any claims to rank among the notable homes of the country. . . . They show him to have no pleasure in noble architecture, to appreciate nothing of the beauty of fine lines and decorations. Mr. Rockefeller's favorite home, the house at Forest Hill, is a monument of cheap ugliness.

In short, he was no "splendid old Venetian" who liked to squander his fortune on palaces and galleries—"so far as the world knows, he is poor in his pleasures." [23] In sum, here was the "money-mad" miser. Reflecting upon these and other paradoxes, E. L. Godkin came to the conclusion that the display expenditures of the rich were "in a certain sense, the product of the popular manners." [24]

Squinting at European precedents with which he was acquainted, Godkin feared that American rich men in building great houses—"slavish imitation"—were making two radical mistakes. Overseas the possession of big

[23] "John D. Rockefeller: A Character Study," *McClure's Magazine*, XXV (July–Aug., 1905), 249, 387.

[24] "The Expenditure of Rich Men," *Scribner's Magazine*, XX (Oct., 1896), 495.

houses had as its "reasons"—the ownership of great territorial possessions and "the practice of hospitality on a scale unknown among us." The owner gathers about him "a large circle of men and women . . . who can talk to each other so as to entertain each other about sport, or art, or literature, or politics," particularly over week ends. In America these precedent conditions were lacking. The owner of the big house might collect people in his drawing room.

But what kind of company would it be? How many of the guests would have anything to say to each other? Suppose "stocks" to be ruled out, where would the topics of conversation be found? Would there be much to talk about except the size of the host's fortune, and that of some other persons present? How many of the men would wish to sit with the ladies in the evening and participate with them in conversation? Would the host attempt two such gatherings, without abandoning his efforts in disgust, selling out the whole concern, and going to Europe? [25]

In spite of its sharpness, this was criticism on a charitable and kindly plane. Much more common was the charge that the big house was not necessary; it was "luxury." Luxurious living was bad, first of all, for those who lived in such a manner. Such houses contributed to "the high tension of life; the temptations it thus opens to business men, goaded to speculation and peculation to keep up with the 'style'; the stimulus it gives to the idle and frivolous and sensuous life of women (and

[25] *Ibid.*, p. 499.

sensuous is not far from sensual)," declared an Episco-
palian minister, spokesman for the social gospel.[26] Lud-
wig Lewisohn in his discussion of Howells' *Rise of Silas
Lapham* has observed that in that generation a girl's
room "seemed terribly intimate. . . . Irene blushed
deeply and turned her head away" when her father
mentioned it.[27] A house with forty bedrooms could not
be pure. Inferences of this sort received factual support
from Jim Fisk, who along with Gould purchased a
marble palace in mid-town New York. This they converted into offices for the Erie Railroad. The palace
also contained an opera house. As Henry Adams observed, "The atmosphere of the Erie offices was not
supposed to be disturbed with moral prejudices; and as
the opera itself supplied Mr. Fisk's mind with amuse-
ment, so the opera *troupe* supplied him with a permanent harem. Whatever Mr. Fisk did was done on an
extraordinary scale." [28] We need not take this example
too seriously. Fisk was not typical, for, according to
James Ford Rhodes, the historian, business to Fisk
"seemed to be a joke." [29] Large houses required paintings; these might make matters much worse. An "esti-
mable family" might even propose "to decorate a

[26] *Report of the Committee* [on Education and Labor] *of the
Senate . . . 1885*, II, 589.

[27] *Expression in America* (New York: Harper, 1932), p. 238.

[28] "The New York Gold Conspiracy," *Westminster Review*,
XCIV (Oct., 1870), 195.

[29] *History of the United States from the Compromise of 1850
to the Final Restoration of Home Rule at the South in 1877* (New
York: Macmillan, 1906), VI, 247.

dining-room ceiling with a copy of the paintings to which the *demi-monde* look up in a celebrated café of Paris." [30] Commodore Vanderbilt's son might outrage the public's notion of railroad responsibility by incautiously saying, "The public be damned," but he took precaution not to give offense in terms of art patronage. The Awakening of Aurora on his wife's bedroom ceiling was not "questionable" since "this imaginative rendering is expressed in figures . . . from which every trace of the empire of carnal sense has been kept away." [31]

In addition to setting a bad example, big houses were also likely to arouse social discontent. Certainly this was not the purpose of their owners, for the houses were not built to impress the groundlings. Chateau row along Fifth Avenue appeared long before the rubberneck busses proceeded up the thoroughfare while the barker's megaphone informed passengers choked by exhaust smoke and carbon monoxide of the accumulated wealth there on display; nor were the cable cars on Nob Hill then built to carry the curious to the summit where they could gape at the castles of railroad and mining kings. Furthermore Newport and Asheville, comparatively speaking, could muster no crowds to gaze at palaces. These palaces were erected to impress one's fellow millionaires. Nonetheless the contrast was there. The young Gifford Pinchot, employed to his delight as a forester on

[30] *Report of the Committee* [on Education and Labor] *of the Senate . . . 1885,* II, 590.
[31] Andrews, *Vanderbilt Legend,* p. 223.

Vanderbilt's Biltmore estate, meditated upon the chateau: "As a feudal castle it would have been beyond criticism, and perhaps beyond praise. But in the United States of the nineteenth century and among the one-room cabins of the Appalachian mountaineers, it did not belong. The contrast was a devastating commentary on the injustice of concentrated wealth." [32] Of course in the burgeoning urban areas the contrast was sharper. The millionaire's palace was at one end of the avenue; the overcrowded tenement at the other. Even the stables of the former cost more and were more comfortable than the latter. [33]

Still it was hard to answer the argument that the construction of the big house employed labor and, by chance, provided patronage for the arts. American architects were backward in providing a counter rationale. Discriminating students of architecture, like Russell Sturgis, Jr., might deliver an occasional obiter dictum to the effect that "ostentation," "mere glitter," and "mere display of costliness" were not avenues to art, [34] but the apostles of the newness in American architecture, in spite of their frequent and loud pronouncements in favor of democracy and the people, rarely provided social criticism of the big house. Louis Sullivan's mirth at the chateau that Richard M. Hunt provided for

[32] Gifford Pinchot, *Breaking New Ground* (New York: Harcourt, Brace, 1947), p. 48.

[33] *Report of the Committee* [on Education and Labor] *of the Senate . . . 1885*, I, 419; II, 403–404, 589.

[34] "Modern Architecture," *North American Review*, CXII (Jan., 1871), 175.

W. K. Vanderbilt on Fifth Avenue was scorn at the chronological inappropriateness of such a building for a "gentleman in a silk hat." [35] Perhaps English critics would make good the deficiency. John Ruskin and William Morris, it was said, had demonstrated that art came out of the people. "Art was not born in the palace; rather she fell sick there, and it will take more bracing air than that of rich men's houses to heal her again." A sound art could arise only from a sound society. And luxury, equivalent to frivolity or selfishness, could not provide a fit environment for "the highest art." That the construction of the big house provided jobs was a "sophistry," that it had aesthetic byproducts might be demonstrated, but Americans needed "genuine aestheticism and not the 'Oscar Wilde' sort." [36]

Actually when struck, allies, like Morris and Ruskin, gave back an uncertain sound. Ruskin advocated no "meanness of private habitation. I would fain introduce into it all magnificence, care, and beauty, where they are possible; but I would not have that *useless* expense in *unnoticed* fineries or formalities." [37] (Italics mine.) William Morris detected the Philistine among all classes and pitied the rich men, who by their failure

---

[35] Andrews, *Vanderbilt Legend*, p. 252.

[36] *Report of the Committee* [on Education and Labor] *of the Senate . . . 1885*, II, 591–592; W. M. Morris, *Hopes and Fears for Art: Five Lectures Delivered in Birmingham, London, and Nottingham, 1878–1881* (London and New York: Longmans, 1896), pp. 189–191.

[37] John Ruskin, *The Seven Lamps of Architecture* (New York: Wiley, 1849), p. 15.

to rise above the "brutality" of the masses "had defrauded themselves as well as the poor," [38] and commended the expenditures of the rich as long as their motives were good. Costliness "is not luxury, if it be done for beauty's sake, and not for show." [39] In view of the contradictions of these English prophets, the impatience of Senator Blair of New Hampshire, chairman of the Senate Committee on Education and Labor, with a witness who claimed Ruskin "has given the best definition of money of any man living" was understandable. Blair replied, "Mr. Ruskin is a fine painter." [40]

In the end, the American attack on the big house fell back upon terms of expediency and morality. On the first count, people of that day were prone to worry about what they called "the dangerous classes." It was said such were more likely to be found in the "private palace" than in the "pestiferous tenement." [41] As for morality, it was wrong for rich men to spend so much money on extravagant housing. Occasionally implicit in this argument was the idea that the money would be better spent for other purposes, perhaps model housing for the poor or some other humanitarian enterprise. "One gorgeous palace absorbs all the labor and expense that might have made a thousand hovels comfortable." [42] So if the millionaire had already demonstrated a philan-

[38] *Op. cit.*, pp. 87–88.   [39] *Ibid.*, p. 110.

[40] *Report of the Committee* [on Education and Labor] *of the Senate . . . 1885*, III, 480.

[41] *Ibid.*, II, 589.

[42] *Twelfth Annual Report of the* [Massachusetts] *Board of Education together with the Twelfth Annual Report of the Secretary of the Board* (Boston: Dutton and Wentworth, 1849), p. 55.

thropic tendency, he could be forgiven an indulgence in the big house. "Who ever would have grudged dear old Peter Cooper the finest house he could have builded." [43] Since it was a common assumption among "philanthropists, Professors, and Lady Millionaires" in this era that there was just so much money around and the real problem of the day was its division, it would be more deserving to devote the funds spent for the large house to the production of decencies for the people rather than "to pad the couch, and pamper the appetite of indolence." [44] Defenders of luxurious expenditures thought the actuality of the situation quite different. If the labor called forth in providing the big house and its appurtenances were devoted to the production of necessities, there would be too much of the latter and the country " 'would be smothered in its own grease'; all might fatten alike upon the gross product of mere animal necessities, without mental development or progress of any kind." [45] Furthermore the implication that the presence of the big house meant the existence of the hovel was unsound. As a Professor of Economics at Boston University snapped, "The notion there is necessarily any causal connection between opulence and poverty is too crude to require serious refutation." [46]

[43] *Report of the Committee* [on Education and Labor] *of the Senate . . . 1885,* II, 591.

[44] John Bascom, *Political Economy: Designed as a Text-book for Colleges* (Andover, Mass.: Warren F. Draper, 1860), pp. 134–135.

[45] Edward Atkinson, "How Can Wages Be Increased?" *Forum,* V (July, 1888), 501.

[46] F. S. Baldwin, "Some Aspects of Luxury," *North American Review,* CLXVIII (Feb., 1899), 160.

However sharp the reproof, the critics of the big house still thought it an evil to be crushed. They were given pause by the realization that the capitalist's bad motives, of selfishness and vanity, nonetheless spurred his productive faculties. "As long as the vanity of wealth is a ruling motive for its acquisition," concluded John Bascom, president of the University of Wisconsin, "we cannot expect nor do the interests of production suffer us to wish that luxury should be restrained, or any more generous impulses be forced on industry, than those of the social state which sustain it. Our remedy is not physical but moral; not in economic regulations, but in enlarged culture." [47] Henry George joined in the aversion to any "sumptuary legislation" on the matter of housing.[48]

Others of a bolder and less thoughtful temper flirted with the idea that at least a ceiling should be placed on the amount a millionaire could spend for a house.[49] However much such direct intervention challenged deep American folkways, there was a strain in American thought which justified it. Prohibition of expenditures for alcohol was often motivated by the concern of the employer with the habits and expenses of his employee and by the concern of the big taxpayer with the expensive maintenance of the chronically inebriated. But was it not true also that the rich drank as much champagne

[47] *Op. cit.*, pp. 136–137.
[48] *Report of the Committee* [on Education and Labor] *of the Senate . . . 1885*, I, 514.
[49] *Ibid.*, I, 265–266.

as the poor did lager beer? [50] Into the clamor of such *tu quoque*'s Atkinson moved with the serenity of his ubiquitous calculations. No matter what he receives in income,

a man costs only what he consumes. . . . The question may well be asked, What class wastes the most, the rich in their luxurious personal expenditure, or the mass of the people who spend a sum variously computed at $700,000,-000 to $1,000,000,000 a year on spirits, beer and tobacco? So far as any computation is possible, in my judgment, the annual product, *i.e.*, the wage and profit fund, is impaired more seriously by the waste of the poor and ignorant, . . . than by all the luxurious expenditure of the rich.[51]

In view of the complexities in preventing a man from spending his money as he pleased, it was more feasible to prevent him from having so much money to spend. Here taxation was the key. The statement of Justice Stephen J. Field in the income tax decision of 1895 that such a tax was "an assault upon capital" has occasioned much derision, then and since. In view of the percentage level of the tax, 2 per cent upon incomes over $4,000, Field's assertion was surely so much an overstatement as to be ludicrous.[52] In all likelihood the many motives which lay behind the statute [53] contained those elements of

[50] *Ibid.*, I, 1164.

[51] Atkinson, "How Can Wages Be Increased?" p. 498.

[52] Sidney Ratner, *American Taxation: Its History as a Social Force in Democracy* (New York: Norton, 1942), pp. 191, 202.

[53] F. P. Summers, *William L. Wilson and Tariff Reform* (New Brunswick: Rutgers University Press, 1953), pp. 168–169, 172–174.

envy and disapproval of the use of wealth which the issue of the big house had raised. "Let those pay the taxes who reap out of the nation more than they need," a laboring man had declared in the previous decade, and a manufacturer would tax the millionaires so heavily that extravagant living would be impossible. "I maintain that a person can go through this life with an income of $25,000 per annum very comfortably." [54]

Clearly such responses came naturally to those whose income was used up in day-by-day expenditures on consumption. They revealed, however, a complete ignorance of the economic order and how it worked. The income of rich men was not usually dissipated in riotous and extravagant living; it was employed in trade and industry. As Charles Elliott Perkins wrote in 1891, the money Huntington and Gould accumulated "does them personally very little good—a small part of their incomes may be wasted in show or champagne, but most of it is invested in some form of industry which directly benefits the masses by making something cheaper." "Natural law" insures that the tendency of wealth is to reproduce itself.[55] According to this school of thought the criticism of the expenditures of rich men, of which the big house was a symbol, was an irrelevance, except for the censorious, the envious, and the merely worried. Within

[54] *Report of the Committee* [on Education and Labor] *of the Senate . . . 1885*, I, 419, 618–623; II, 38; Topics of the Time, "Shall Fortunes Be Limited by Law?" *Century Illustrated Magazine*, XXXV (April, 1888), 963–964.

[55] Letter to T. M. Marquett, Jan. 3, 1891, Perkins Private Letters and Memos, R.C.O.

the business community, nonetheless, there was occasional uneasiness at the current architectural exhibitionism. Carnegie, with the cosmic air he customarily gave to his utterances, held forth upon the historical disadvantages of "long-continued prosperity," the chief of which was "the reign of luxury and the vices it breeds." Great Britain had already entered that phase.[56] With civilization had come "the contrast between the palace and the cottage of the laborer." Since this was the necessary price for progress, it is "the duty of the man of Wealth: First to set an example of modest, unostentatious living, shunning display or extravagance." [57] It is true "the star-spangled Scotchman" had no yacht, no opera box, no old masters and first editions. But he did have a home with a garden and lawn on upper Fifth Avenue, and a castle in Scotland on an estate of 32,000 acres.[58] Like Atkinson, Carnegie knew that millionaires must cost something.

[56] Andrew Carnegie, "The Industrial Ascendancy of the World," in B. J. Hendrick, ed., *Miscellaneous Writings of Andrew Carnegie* (New York: Doubleday, 1933), I, 103.

[57] "Wealth," *North American Review*, CXLVIII (June, 1889), 653, 661.

[58] Hendrick, *Life of Andrew Carnegie*, II, 147–150, 259, 269.

III

The Political Economy
of the Public School

MR. GOMPERS, long-time head of the American Federation of Labor and founder of the modern organized labor movement in the United States, committed himself on one occasion to the following view of educational history: "Organized labor has always stood for, aye, has been the pioneer in the demand for free schools, free textbooks, compulsory education in the elementary grades and for the fullest and freest opportunity in all lines of learning, technology included." [1]

[1] *American Federationist,* Dec., 1909, quoted in P. R. V. Curoe, *Educational Attitudes and Policies of Organized Labor in the United States* (New York: Teachers College, Columbia University, 1926), p. 7.

Some historians have gone beyond Gompers and asserted that the American free public school, the crowning glory of the American heritage, had emerged almost exclusively from the workingmen, organized or unorganized, albeit they vouchsafed a place in the process to general reformers, who like us not, for instance Fanny Wright, operated through the labor movement.[2] Though others have doubted this simplistic historical explanation, few have made bold to question the concomitant thesis that the men of wealth and of business have, in general, been suspicious of the free school movement. This class, it is said, possessed the means to educate its own children and were unwilling to pay increased taxes called for by a state-supported system which would educate the poor. The argument ran further: free schooling for the less well to do "would result in the loss of their self-respect and initiative" and give people ambitions or talents beyond their station.[3] Finally the free public school system defied certain natural rights—justice in the distribution of taxes and the prerogative of the parent to educate his child as he wished. In short, on the matter of democratic education wealth and business was selfish, obscurantist, callous, and indifferent.

This clash of doctrine—and the inferences drawn from it—has usually been assigned to the period before

[2] F. T. Carlton, *Economic Influences upon Educational Progress in the United States, 1820–1850* (Bull. of the University of Wisconsin, No. 221; Madison, 1908), *passim.*

[3] Merle Curti, *The Growth of American Thought* (New York: Harper, 1943), p. 351.

the Civil War. Apparently the arguments continued into the era after that conflict. E. E. White, long-time Commissioner of Education of Ohio and the president who really got Purdue University under way, in 1881 informed his readers, with the verbal magic so common to educationalists, that there were three aristocracies, those of Caste, Capital, and Culture, opposing the education of the people. The second, the aristocracy of Capital, "asserts that popular education is a tax on capital. The more intelligent a man is the greater are his wants and the higher must be his wages in order to meet his increased necessities. Ignorant labor has few wants to supply, and hence is content with low wages." [4] And B. G. Northrup, Secretary of the Board of Education of Connecticut, about the same time was informing a congressional committee that, "a few men of wealth, without children, complain of the injustice of being compelled to pay for the education of others." [5] Current changes in the public school system undoubtedly vitalized these traditional objections. For one thing the kindergarten was extending the school system at the lower end and the high school at the upper: for another, attendance was no longer voluntary, law was making it compulsory. "If the State has the right to compel the childless

[4] E. E. White, "The Relation of Education to Industry," *Circulars of the* [U.S.] *Bureau of Education*, No. 2, 1881, p. 14.

[5] Statements and Testimony of the Committee of State Superintendents of Public Instruction in National and the Common Schools, Hearing before the Committee of the Senate on Education and Labor and the House Committee on Education, 1884, in 48 Cong., 1 Sess., *Sen. Misc. Docs.*, No. 55 (s.n. 2171), p. 81.

rich to pay for the education of the children of the people," an educator informed his colleagues, "the State has the right to compel them to accept it." [6]

As this utterance hints, the arguments of many educationalists in behalf of current educational changes were poorly calculated to reassure those who believed in self-help and individual freedom or were inclined to be wary of governmental enterprise. Rather, brain-bathed by German thought, particularly that of Hegel, or by their own educational experience in Germany, these educators talked and wrote extravagantly of the welfare of the State and of the State's *"right of eminent domain"* over the "minds and souls and bodies" of the individual. In this context, education "cannot be left to the caprices and contingencies of individuals, or even of associated effort and enterprise. . . . It is too gigantic for private capital; too momentous for the mischances of private judgement. The commonwealth, in its strong and benign sovereignty, must stretch forth its arm and do this thing." [7] Nor did educational proposals of this era merely ruffle ideas commonly held by businessmen; they touched their economic interests by encroaching upon the employment of children in industry and business and by featuring the advantages of diminishing hours of work in favor of intellectual pursuits—and, of course, it is well known that employers were convinced of the

[6] *The Addresses and Journal of Proceedings of the National Educational Association . . . 1871* (New York & Washington: James H. Holmes, 1872), p. 222.

[7] Newton Bateman, "How Far May the State Provide for the Education of Her Children at Public Cost?" *N.E.A. Proceedings, 1871*, pp. 26–27.

wisdom and necessity of child labor and of excessive work periods.

On the other hand, perceptive educators repeatedly pointed out to men of business and wealth the advantages of education. It would in the first place abate the hostility between labor and capital. "There is offered here in America the fairest field for the successful solution of every irritating question arising between capital and labor," wrote the National Commissioner of Education in 1870, "without conflict, without harm to either, without a disturbance of the great harmonies necessary to the highest national prosperity. But reason cannot exercise its sway without knowledge, nor knowledge be possible without the means for its acquisition." [8] For generalizations of this order, the great railroad strikes of 1877, including the Pittsburgh riot, provided examples. On this traumatic theme educators harped over the years. In 1877 the Commissioner of Education was in a put-up or shut-up mood. "All the powers" of the child, he wrote, "must be developed to resist misfortune and wrong. Capital, therefore, should weigh the cost of the mob and the tramp against the expense of universal and sufficient education." [9]

[8] *Circular of Information of the* [U.S.] *Bureau of Education for April, 1872*, p. 15; *Report of the* [Massachusetts] *Bureau of Statistics of Labor . . . from March 1, 1870 to March 1, 1871* (Boston: Wright & Potter, 1871), pp. 28–31, 461, 464.

[9] *Report of the* [U.S.] *Commissioner of Education . . . 1877*, p. viii; *N.E.A. Proceedings, 1877* (Salem, Ohio: Allan K. Tatem, 1877), p. 6; *Report of the Committee* [on Education and Labor] *of the Senate upon the Relations between Labor and Capital, 1885*, II, 153–154.

That these arguments impressed the business community as a whole is doubtful. In some instances business observers expressed a belief that education was a bulwark for property, for law and order.[10] In others they felt that education stimulated discontent, for it heightened desires which neither individual capacity nor the level of the economy was able to gratify; by inculcating a knowledge of writing and figuring it enabled workers to perceive and calculate their grievances; it might make them more redoubtable foes in labor struggles.[11] Opinions of this latter sort inspired one derisive commentator from Wisconsin to assert:

We believe that education is one of the principal causes of the discontent of late years manifesting itself among the laboring classes, and would therefore favor the abolishment of the public school system. . . . Turn the school fund over to the churches, and make attendance at divine worship, of the laboring classes, compulsory. Compel clergymen to preach principally about Lazarus and the rich man; about the camel trying to crawl through the eye of a needle, &c.; that Vanderbilt, Jay Gould, Alexander Mitchel, and all rich men will surely go to hell when they die; that the pay of "skilled workmen" at the building of Solomon's temple was a penny a day and no grumbling allowed.[12]

[10] *Report of the Committee* [on Education and Labor] *of the Senate . . . 1885*, I, 1089–1090.

[11] *Ibid.*, II, 909, 1099–1100; *Circular of Information of the* [U.S.] *Bureau of Education for April, 1872*, pp. 25, 26.

[12] *Report of the Committee* [on Education and Labor] *of the Senate . . . 1885*, II, 1382–1383.

Be this wit or not, it certainly was misleading. Actually only the minority of the business community preferred ignorance to education as a prerequisite for contented workers. A representative of the workers provided the soundest evidence: "While abroad I have heard boss-mechanics argue against their employés having too much education, as they thought ignorance made them better satisfied to remain mere servile drudges, and I have heard sentiments similar in my own country, but, thank God, seldom." [13]

More effective with the business community than the argument of education aiding law and order, was the appeal to its direct self-interest: educated workers were more productive and efficient. The latter were able to comprehend instruction and proceed in their work on their own responsibility, thus saving expense in the matter of superintendence and direction, a critical factor in the organization of laborers in an enlarged scale of enterprise; educated workers were less wasteful and more ingenious in solving the problems of doing their task more easily and at less cost; they were also more industrious and less dissipated. One of the classic attempts at this argument had been made by Horace Mann in 1846, when he was secretary of the Massachusetts Board of Public Education.[14] In the post-Civil War era, the cogency of Mann's demonstration was still remem-

[13] *Circular of Information of the* [U.S.] *Bureau of Education for April, 1872*, p. 55.

[14] *Tenth Annual Report of the* [Massachusetts] *Board of Education, together with the Tenth Annual Report of the Secretary of the Board* (Boston: Dutton and Wentworth, 1847), pp. 202–203.

bered.[15] Perhaps on the ground that things had changed and businessmen outside of Massachusetts might not be so enlightened, the National Commissioner of Education in 1870 dispatched a series of eight questions dealing with education and labor to a sample of employers, workingmen, and general observers.[16] The questions, since they were formulated without benefit of modern techniques for objectivity, were certainly loaded. A deep obscurity also shrouds the process by which the Commissioner's office was able to quantify random replies into a percentage figure; but in any case his annual report asserted the increase of wages the worker would receive "on account of his knowledge" averaged near 25 per cent.[17] Here also occasion provided supporting argument.

Throughout the decades after the Civil War, there was a deliberate effort on the part of American producers to learn as much as possible of the reasons for the industrial greatness of other nations, particularly Great Britain, and to shape their policy and objectives accordingly. To those concerned with the qualifications necessary for success in the international industrial arena, the Paris Exposition of 1867 was instructive, for the judges of the products reached a verdict that

Great Britain has excelled her competitors in but ten of all [ninety] departments. The announcement of this verdict

[15] *Report of the Committee* [on Education and Labor] *of the Senate . . . 1885,* III, 309–310.

[16] *Report of the* [U.S.] *Commissioner of Education . . . 1870,* pp. 39–40.

[17] *Ibid.,* p. 51.

produced consternation among the representatives of British industry. They met at the Hôtel du Louvre, and the one absorbing inquiry was, "Why this defeat?" The unexpected news crossed the channel, causing greater alarm than the threatened invasion by Napoleon I. This defeat awakened England to the startling fact that the industrial sceptre was slipping from her hands; and, as a result, she saw her ships rotting in her harbors, and the hammer falling from the hand of her starving workmen. The disaster arrested public attention, and a searching and thorough investigation for its cause was made by a Parliamentary commission. The report made to Parliament in 1868 contains the testimony and the conclusion. *Education had won the palm of excellence for her competitors.*[18]

Whether in accord with the facts or not, at least this was the version presented to American readers by the president of Purdue University. In the nineties the Spanish-American War and the resulting acquisition of "dominion over palm and pine" gave a new gloss to the interrelationships between education and economic affairs. Pleading for business education, J. H. Francis announced in 1899, "The struggle of the future will not be on the battlefields, but in the arena of trades, markets, and exchanges." [19] In the same decade the widespread unemployment during the depression of 1893–1897 and the industrial armies wandering about the country in search of some sort of relief, led the president of the Throop Polytechnic Institute at Pasadena to correlate

[18] White, "The Relation of Education to Industry," p. 18.
[19] "The Claims of Business Education to a Place in our Public Schools," *N.E.A. Proceedings, 1899* (Chicago: The Association, 1899), p. 1011.

this disturbing idleness with an absence of technical training. "The great itinerant army of the unemployed is an army of untrained men." [20]

To arguments such as these, the business community, however it might differ on details, gave a well-nigh universal and continuous affirmation. Indeed its spokesmen provided a good share of the argument itself. The manager of the American Standard Tool Company at Newark, New Jersey, was typical when, in 1870, he said, "Knowledge is wealth, where skill is exercised with fidelity and honor, in a manufacturing business at least." [21] Textile manufacturers from Massachusetts agreed: "Everything is in favor of the educated and intelligent," and "I never had an educated man or woman in my employ who was not worth to me in any employment more than one who was not educated. The more they know the better they work." [22] In the middle eighties the same theme was repeated to a Senate committee: "Intelligence pays. There is nothing like intelligence in manufacturing." [23]

In its argument for education, the business commu-

[20] C. H. Keyes, "The Modifications of Secondary School Courses Most Demanded by the Conditions of Today and Most Ignored by the Committee of Ten," *N.E.A. Proceedings, 1895* (St. Paul: The Association, 1895), p. 740.

[21] *Report of the* [U.S.] *Commissioner of Education . . . 1870,* p. 451.

[22] *Circular of Information of the* [U.S.] *Bureau of Education for April, 1872,* pp. 35, 41.

[23] *Report of the Committee* [on Education and Labor] *of the Senate . . . 1885,* III, 309.

nity sometimes groped toward a more fundamental rationalization. Ignorance was a prison; education struck off the shackles. It both freed and helped men more effectively to help themselves. Thus, though it originally involved effort and expense—and even compulsion—on the part of the state, it eventually made possible a limitation of state action.[24] The most influential educational thinker of that day, W. T. Harris, thus analyzed the theory of American education:

Not only is this the land of individuality, but we are living in an age of individuality. . . . *We* desire in our systems of education to make the citizen as independent as possible from mere external prescriptions. We wish him to be spontaneous—self-active—self-governing. . . . We give the pupil the conventionalities of a perpetual self-education. With the tools to work with . . . he can unfold indefinitely his latent powers. . . . The pride of America is her self-educated men. . . . Indeed an edict has gone forth to the New World in our Declaration of Independence: "Woe unto that head which cannot govern its pair of hands" Unto the lower races who fail in this, it reads the sentence: "If you cannot direct your own hands by your own intelligence you only encumber the ground here, and can remain by sufferance in this place only so long as land is cheap." [25]

[24] *Ibid.*, pp. 325, 351, 436.
[25] "The Theory of American Education," *Addresses and Journal of Proceedings of the American Normal School, and the National Teachers' Associations . . . 1870* (Washington: James H. Holmes, 1871), pp. 188, 189, 191; W. T. Harris, "The Curriculum for Secondary Schools," *Report of the* [U.S.] *Commissioner of Education for 1892–1893*, II, 1460, 1461.

Of course it is possible to argue that affirmations of this sort were not the decisive factors in winning the allegiance of the business community to public education. Perhaps that community was canny enough to realize in the latter part of the century that opposition was futile. For instance, in 1870 the officials of a rubber works in Trenton, New Jersey, announced they were "all in favor of education and mental culture: should any one doubt this in this age?" [26]

A speaker before the educators of the nation in convention assembled summarized in 1871 the historic American justification for education at public expense:

A free republican commonwealth . . . is grounded, of necessity, first, upon those universal and immutable maxims of truth and right which underlie the thought of Christendom; and second, upon a clear translation of those fundamental maxims into the forms of written constitutions and laws. These must be understood, to be of any worth in the maintenance of the State—understood by *all*, to be of the highest worth, of absolute saving power to the State. But how can they be understood except they be read? How understood by all, except read by all? . . . [The State] must teach its children to read. [27]

Formulated in an earlier day, these twin objectives of Religion and Patriotism still had overpowering relevance in the years after the Civil War. To begin with,

[26] *Report of the* [U.S.] *Commissioner of Education . . . 1870*, p. 452.

[27] Bateman, *op. cit.*, p. 26.

that conflict emancipated the Negro and gave him the ballot; the ignorant black must be educated to be an intelligent voter. These were also the decades of immigrants. They had to be Americanized and, if illiterate, made literate. "Remember," wrote a Massachusetts manufacturer, "that with us the uneducated are foreigners." [28] While businessmen, as American citizens, might feel the necessity of an education to perform these historic tasks, they also had needs of their own.

The establishment of new industries and the expansion or diversification of old ones depended upon the availability of skilled workers, for in its industrial phase, the nation was then nearer the days of Samuel Slater and the Scholfields than those of automation. The shortage of skilled workers was hard to surmount. For one thing apprenticeship as a means of training was dead; there were almost as many reasons for its demise as for the death of Cock Robin, and censures flew thick and fast. [29] They could not resuscitate the corpse. One way to meet the handicap was to import skills from abroad, and old industries like textiles depended upon immigrants for their designers, dyers, and engravers, and the domestication of new industries, like tin-plating, required a wholesale transfer of skilled workers across the At-

[28] *Circular of the* [U.S.] *Bureau of Education for April, 1872,* p. 35.

[29] *Report of the Committee* [on Education and Labor] *of the Senate . . . 1885,* II, 987; L. S. Thompson, "The Decay of Apprenticeship: Its Cause and Remedies," *N.E.A. Proceedings, 1881* (Salem, Ohio: A. K. Tatem, 1881), pp. 246–248.

lantic.[30] So commonplace was this practice that some employers thought those who wanted to stop such reliance a little silly, as the following colloquy between employers revealed.

For example, one man said to me, "Why do you want a technical school?" I said, "because if I want a draftsman or foreman I want a well-equipped man, and I can't get him in the ordinary workman, unless he has had some opportunities of acquiring knowledge that he cannot get in a shop." "Well, is that the only reason? You could send abroad and get all that in men who have been trained in technical schools already established." [31]

While it might be practical thus to avoid the bother and expense of training workmen in this country, the nationalist cast of thought, most prominently represented in the protective tariff, was not willing to approve. Joseph Medill, editor of the Chicago *Tribune*, thought importation of foreign artisans was "all wrong. It is a cruel injustice to the rising generation of Americans and a source of weakness to the body politic." [32] A Boston agent for many textile mills agreed that American youths should have the right to be industrially educated. He added, "We have something to fall back upon

[30] R. T. Berthoff, *British Immigrants in Industrial America, 1790–1950* (Cambridge: Harvard University Press, 1955), pp. 68–69; *Report of the Committee* [on Education and Labor] *of the Senate . . . 1885*, III, 373–374.

[31] *Report of the Committee* [on Education and Labor] *of the Senate . . . 1885*, II, 1129.

[32] *Ibid.*, p. 964.

if we are short of designers. Sometimes we are obliged to go to Europe to get them, which is very inconvenient, and it is a great deal better for our manufacturing interests to produce them at home if possible." [33] Those suspicious of the motives of anyone who had a few thousand dollars fell easily into the belief that of course employers were eager to have the youngsters trained to increase the number of workers and, through the law of supply and demand, thus lower wages and costs. Employers believed that expanding industry would take care of the trained recruits, if there were not too many of them, like bookkeepers,[34] and would have been quite bewildered at the conception that it was disadvantageous for any individual to have a "trade," skills, or educated talents.

Motives aside, there arose "a constant clamor for the 'practical'" in education.[35] To assume on *a priori* grounds that the guild of teachers and administrators was a group willing to ally itself with this business objective is to invite being misled. On the contrary, both interest and idealism pulled most educators the other way. On the first count, new subjects might well mean technological unemployment for those trained to teach the old ones. On ideological grounds teachers were the

[33] *Ibid.*, III, 311; *Circular of Information of the* [U.S.] *Bureau of Education for April, 1872,* p. 106.

[34] *Report of the Committee* [on Education and Labor] *of the Senate . . . 1885,* III, 14.

[35] E. Mackey, discussing a paper on "Education for the Industrial Classes," *N.E.A. Proceedings, 1898* (Chicago: University of Chicago Press, 1898), p. 764.

heirs of a traditional culture which was somewhat leery of those making a living. According to two of the pedagogues' most gifted spokesmen, Nicholas Murray Butler and Charles W. Eliot, the philosophers of the glory that was Greece held ideas about education quite different from those of late nineteenth-century businessmen. According to Butler, Aristotle had a preference for a sort of education which was not "useful or necessary" but "liberal and noble," and according to Eliot, Plato "maintained that the producing or industrial classes needed no education." [36] On the whole American educators agreed. They maintained, "We must educate away from the controlling forces of society, on the ground that those forces and conditions are not ideal, and it is the business of education to strive for the ideal." [37]

Whether the guild spirit of educators was defense enough against business pressure depended upon the sector of the school system. One of the educational innovations of the era, the kindergarten, roused little business antipathy. Its emphasis on training in color and form and on the manipulation of material was, on the contrary, all to the good in the minds of those convinced that the eye and hand must be trained rather than neglected. Then came the elementary and grammar school,

[36] N. M. Butler, "The Reform of Secondary Education in the United States" and C. W. Eliot, "The Unity of Educational Reforms," *Report of the* [U.S.] *Commissioner of Education for 1892–1893*, II, 1456, 1465.

[37] Francis, *op. cit.*, p. 1012; D. W. Springer, "Business Education," *N.E.A. Proceedings, 1898*, pp. 858–859.

the "common schools." Business accepted them. These were the schools which gave a training in the three R's, along with spelling and geography. They were the schools which gave also a training for citizenship. Furthermore they were the schools which had come down to us from the "original founders" of the school system and had thus a sort of historical sanctity.[38] The admittedly crowded curriculum of these years might be shortened by omitting the memorization of facts better looked up in a gazetteer, the exercises of arithmetic which bewildered and exhausted pupils, and the puzzles in grammar.[39] This saved time should be used for physical education. "The large majority of those, who are under our care must earn their bread in the sweat of their brow. Such is God's decree. To this end their bodily powers are of vast moment, and the pains of a life of toil may be allayed or mitigated by such physical condition as shall secure an easy and it may be pleasurable exercise of these powers."[40] The saved time should be used also for drawing, which by its emphasis on attention, accuracy, and the perception of form "eminently

[38] *Report of the* [U.S.] *Commissioner of Education . . . 1877*, p. lxxxi.

[39] L. S. Thompson, "Relations of the Common School to Industrial Education," *N.E.A. Proceedings, 1877*, pp. 219–220; *Report of the Committee* [on Education and Labor] *of the Senate . . . 1885*, III, 337–338.

[40] J. L. Pickard, "The Human Body, A Subject of Study for the Teacher," *Addresses and Journal of Proceedings of the American Normal School, and the National Teachers' Associations . . . 1870*, p. 43.

deserves the name of 'breadwinner' " ("Massachusetts, with a never-failing instinct as to how money is to be made, has passed a law [in 1870], *requiring* drawing"),[41] for manual training, for geometry ("if the theoretical side is exclusively taught we shall make scientists; if the practical side, we may do something towards helping practical workmen"), and for natural science, especially physics and chemistry.[42]

If expediency prevented doing much to harmonize the grade schools with an age of steam and electricity, if even the moderate changes accomplished could be interpreted as cultural rather than practical, as "general education" rather than particularized instruction— manual training trained the head through the hand, for "motion is the dawn of the soul" [43]—the high school was in a more vulnerable position to business pressures. Here was a new period of instruction for which, if I may lapse into the educational vernacular for a minute, an educational concept had been institutionalized before it was implemented. It was not the first nor the last time. These four years, now that the rudiments of an education had been secured, now that citizens had been trained, were to provide the education for the leaders.

[41] L. S. Thompson, "Some Reasons Why Drawing Should be Taught in Our Public Schools," *N.E.A. Proceedings, 1877*, pp. 41–43, 44, 50.

[42] L. S. Thompson, "The Decay of Apprenticeship," pp. 247–250; *Report of the* [U.S.] *Commissioner of Education . . . 1870*, p. 450.

[43] F. J. White, "Physical Effects of Sloyd," *N.E.A. Proceedings, 1896* (Chicago: University of Chicago Press, 1896), p. 760.

To the educator, it seemed natural that the student should now proceed to the higher reaches of the studies he had already begun, going on to algebra from arithmetic, and initiate the study of new subjects, like the languages. High school was to serve as a transition to college, then admittedly an institution stressing culture. As time went on, the business community found two faults with this decision. To begin with, the subjects taught were of little use in the practical affairs of life. Thus a woolen manufacturer of Wales, Massachusetts, replied to the national Commissioner of Education as to whether he could employ workers with "a higher degree of education," "Don't think we could operate our mills with such a class of help, as we could not run it by algebra." The same informant also preferred workers with only a common-school education since "the more learned are endeavoring to fit themselves for Congress." [44]

This quip unveiled the real core of the charges against the high school. Henry Carey Baird, an industrial publisher of Philadelphia, was not writing with a vehemence exceptional among businessmen when he declared,

Too much education of a certain sort, such as Greek, Latin, French, German, and especially book-keeping, to a person of humble antecedents, is utterly demoralizing in nine cases out of ten, and is productive of an army of mean-spirited "gentlemen" who are above what is called a "trade" and who are only content to follow some such occupation as

[44] *Circular of Information of the* [U.S.] *Bureau of Education for April, 1872,* p. 41.

that of standing behind a counter, and selling silks, gloves, bobbins, or laces, or to "keep books." After a good deal of observation, and more especially during thirteen years past that I have been a pretty close student of social science, I have arrived at the conclusion that our system of education, as furnished by law, when it goes beyond what in Pennsylvania is called a grammar school, is vicious in the extreme—productive of more evil than good. Were the power lodged with me, no boy or girl should be educated at the public expense beyond what he or she could obtain at a grammar school, except for some useful occupation. "The high school" of today must, as I believe, under an enlightened system, be supplanted by *the technical school*, with possibly "shops" connected with it. . . . We are manufacturing too many "gentlemen" and "ladies," so called and demoralization is the result. What good do Greek, Latin, French, German, &c., do to a counter-skipper in a retail dry goods shop? . . . Were I in the position of General Eaton [National Commissioner of Education] I would commence a crusade against the ignorance of our educators, and I would bring the people to a proper recognition of *"what knowledge is most worth,"* as Herbert Spencer has so well and truly sung.[45]

What the business community, if their most articulate members are to be believed, thought the fundamental objective of public school training should be was "character." Professor Thurber of the University of Chicago in the nineties questioned a group of Chicago busi-

[45] *Report of the* [U.S.] *Commissioner of Education . . . 1870*, p. 459; *Report of the Committee* [on Education and Labor] *of the Senate . . . 1885*, II, 964; III, 296.

nessmen about their ideas on education. His informants esteemed the discipline and control of the mind as of more value than the amount of knowledge gained in school.[46] Charles Elliott Perkins in his directions for hiring and promoting employees on the Chicago, Burlington and Quincy Railroad, laid down a series of priorities. "The first question should be, What is the man? What is his character? What are his habits? and then, if these are believed to be good, what has been his education." [47] The facets of the ideal character were many: accuracy, neatness, promptness, fidelity to the interests of employers, a willingness to work and to get hands and clothes dirty, a realization that labor is the source of wealth and is inherently "dignified." The chief trait must be a hardening of the will to fit it for the executive, directive, and administrative tasks. The era had a word for it, "gumption." [48]

Sincere as this allegiance to character as the purpose of education might be, businessmen were not aware that this emphasis weakened their demand for training in

[46] C. H. Thurber, "Is the Present High School Course a Satisfactory Preparation for Business? If Not, How Should It Be Modified?" *N.E.A. Proceedings, 1897* (Chicago: University of Chicago Press, 1897), p. 811.

[47] C. E. Perkins, Memo on the Selection of Employees, August 15, 1885, Perkins Private Letters and Memos, R.C.O.

[48] 48 Cong., 1 Sess., *Senate Misc. Docs.*, No. 55 (s.n. 2171), pp. 9–10; E. E. White, "Technical Training in American Schools," *Circulars of the* [U.S.] *Bureau of Education*, No. 2, 1881, p. 13; C. W. Eliot, "The Unity of Educational Reform," *op. cit.*, p. 1468; Edward Atkinson, *The Industrial Progress of the Nation* (New York: Putnam, 1890), p. 21.

subjects of practical value. Unwittingly they dragged a Trojan horse filled with other-minded educators within their fortress. How could training in morals and character be brought about? In an educational vacuum the best means of such instruction was Christianity and the Bible; [49] in practice the application of this theory raised the "Bible question," which, in the face of America's multiplicity of sects, including the Roman Catholics, had haunted and bedeviled American educational history for decades. Educators might rationalize into the night and seek to dilute the issue until it seemed merely secular—E. E. White declared that in the schools religion is not an end but a means; morality is the end of school training, religion is only a means to the end [50]— but few foes were deceived or diverted. So the path to character was through those studies which had traditionally trained it. Latin, Greek, and mathematics were the ways by which students had developed observation, memory, judgment, and reasoning powers. Few made the charge that this faculty psychology was antiquated and discredited; fewer still paid any attention to these dissents.[51]

In 1893 the famous Committee of Ten of the National

[49] A. D. Mayo, "Methods of Moral Instruction in Common Schools," *N.E.A. Proceedings, 1872* (Peoria, Illinois: N. C. Nason, 1873), pp. 12–13, 20–21.

[50] E. E. White, "Religion in the School," *Proceedings of the International Congress of Education of the World's Columbian Exposition, Chicago, July 25–28, 1893* (New York: The National Educational Association, 1894), pp. 296–297.

[51] "Discussion on the Report of the Committee of Ten," *N.E.A. Proceedings, 1894* (St. Paul: The Association, 1895), p. 162.

Educational Association submitted its decisive report on the desirable courses in high school. Headed by Charles W. Eliot, president of Harvard University, the ninety members of the central committee and the nine subcommittees were guilefully chosen from teachers and administrators, colleges and schools, public and private, and various regions of the country.[52] Their report, characterized by one superintendent of schools as an "educational encyclical," [53] recommended four four-year courses, the classical, the Latin-scientific, modern languages, and English, for the well-bred high school. The preferences of the committee protruded in several paragraphs.

Although the committee thought it expedient to include among the four programmes one which included neither Latin nor Greek, and one which included only one foreign language, . . . they desired to affirm expressly their unanimous opinion that, under existing conditions in the United States as to the training of teachers and the provision of necessary means of instruction, the two programmes called respectively modern languages and English must in practice be distinctly inferior to the other two.[54]

The committee patronizingly informed the advocates of more instruction in natural science and natural history, economy, and geography, that while it was natural for them to desire ardently "to have their respective subjects made equal to Latin, Greek, and mathematics in

[52] "Report of the Committee of Ten on Secondary School Studies," *Report of the* [U.S.] *Commissioner of Education . . . 1892–93*, II, 1416, 1418–1420.

[53] "Discussion on the Report of the Committee of Ten," p. 156.

[54] "Report of the Committee of Ten," pp. 1441–1442.

weight and influence in the schools; . . . they knew that educational tradition was adverse to this desire, and that many teachers and directors of education felt no confidence in these subjects as disciplinary material." [55]

In view of these biases, it was not surprising that the committee took a most Olympian view toward the long agitation for industrial, technical, or trade education and toward business instruction. Drawing was reduced to the handmaid of history and natural science; economics was to be taught in connection with English and history. Bookkeeping and commercial arithmetic might be substituted for algebra, and "if it were desired to provide more amply for subjects thought to have a practical importance in trade and the useful arts," such options could be substituted for natural science in the last two years of the "English programme." [56] How much more inferior this made an already inferior course deponent saith not! Whether they knew it or not, the business community and their allies in the world of education were rapped sharply over the knuckles for their aspirations. Once again mind conquered matter, and Caesar conquered not only Gaul but the turning lathe and the typewriter. The committee preferred to informational studies those which gave mental and moral training.[57] It was little consolation to discern among the committee's magisterial pronouncements a recommendation that in teach-

[55] *Ibid.*, p. 1421.   [56] *Ibid.*, p. 1443.

[57] J. C. MacKenzie, "The Feasibility of Modifying the Programs of the Elementary and Secondary Schools to Meet the Suggestions in the Report of the Committee of Ten," *N.E.A. Proceedings, 1894*, pp. 148–149.

ing English less emphasis be placed on rhetoric and grammar and more on writing English.[58]

In the tradition of self-help which they were always exalting, it was possible for men of means to establish schools to their liking. Although the advocates of culture captured the high school, there were not lacking schoolmen to point out that as a cultural instrument it had so many shortcomings that philanthropists should continue to establish or support the private academy.[59] On the other hand, in view of the need for training in practical affairs, private philanthropy should establish technical, mechanical, manual, or trade schools. A "noble" precedent was at hand from the fifties, when Peter Cooper, "a mechanic of New York" who had acquired a fortune, built and opened Cooper Union "for the advancement of Science and Art." The institution in its aims and curriculum was to make good the deficiency in existing schools, where students left their studies ready to be "anything but workers in the world; so the idea of becoming a skilled artisan, a producer of something, is viewed with contempt." He hoped his institution would be "a polytechnic school of the most thorough character and the highest order, based as nearly as possible upon the model of L'École Centrale at Paris." [60] Other businessmen looked upon this institution with verbal benevolence, and at the century's

[58] "Report of the Committee of Ten," p. 1425.

[59] H. K. Edson, "Classical Study and the Means of Securing It in the West," *N.E.A. Proceedings, 1871*, pp. 161–164.

[60] E. C. Mack, *Peter Cooper: Citizen of New York* (New York: Duell, Sloan and Pearce, 1949), pp. 243–268.

end Andrew Carnegie and Henry H. Rogers gave it $850,000 to realize its preliminary potentialities.[61] European precedents also influenced Charles O. Thompson, who became the first principal of the Worcester County Free Institute of Industrial Science established in the sixties through the generosity of Worcester capitalists for instructing youth between fourteen and twenty-one

in those branches of education not usually taught in the public schools, which are essential, and best adapted to train the young for practical life; and especially, that such as are intending to be mechanics, or manufacturers, or farmers, may attain an understanding of the principles of science applicable to their pursuits which shall qualify them in the best manner for an intelligent and successful prosecution of their business; and that such as intend to devote themselves to any branches of mercantile business, shall in like manner be instructed in those parts of learning most serviceable to them.[62]

All over the country private benefactions established or supported the pioneer schools for manual training.[63]

[61] *Report of the Committee* [on Education and Labor] *of the Senate . . . 1885*, II, 1156; A. S. Hewitt, "Commencement Address at Cooper Union, 1902," Allan Nevins, ed., *Selected Writings of Abram S. Hewitt* (New York: Columbia University Press, 1937), p. 342.

[62] *Worcester County Free Institute of Industrial Science, Addresses of Inauguration and Dedication, Worcester, November 11, 1868, Memorial Notice of John Boynton, Esq., Founder of the Institute, Memorial Notice of Hon. Ichabod Washburn, Founder of the Practical Mechanical Department* (Worcester: Charles Hamilton, 1869), pp. 8–11.

[63] J. E. Hoyt, "Manual Training in the Public Schools of the Smaller Cities," *N.E.A. Proceedings, 1896*, p. 771.

The union of commercial and industrial training at Worcester was unusual; for generally speaking the attainment of industrial training came first. Observers given to dating phenomena in terms of international exhibitions correlate trade schools with the Centennial Exposition of 1876 at Philadelphia. In that year the National Educational Association, a great educational holding company, also recognized facts by establishing an "Industrial Department" for its members.[64] A further reason for making distinctions between trade and business education was that businessmen in productive enterprises were scornful of bookkeeping and equated bookkeepers with undesirable citizens. "Multitudes of farmers' and mechanics' sons seek to be salesmen, clerks, book-keepers, drummers for trade houses, and, failing to find or retain such situations, they become 'sports,' billiard-markers, bar-tenders, confidence men, dead-beats—anything, in short, but hand-soiling working-men." [65] The evolution of commercial instruction thus followed different lines.

These schools were not eleemosynary but proprietary, or, as the proponents of business colleges constantly stressed, they were "private and unendowed." [66] They taught bookkeeping, commercial arithmetic and com-

[64] *N.E.A. Proceedings, 1876* (Salem, Ohio: A. K. Tatem, 1876), pp. 238–240.

[65] *Report of the Committee* [on Education and Labor] *of the Senate . . . 1885*, II, 964; *Report of the* [U.S.] *Commissioner of Education . . . 1870*, p. 459.

[66] S. S. Packard, "Business Education: Its Place in the American Curriculum," *N.E.A. Proceedings, 1892* (New York: The Association, 1893), p. 464.

mercial law, stenography and typewriting, after the typewriter had done away with the need for a "business hand." [67] They came into being because "the great law of supply and demand operates as truly and as surely in the province of the humanities and education as in the realm of economics." Institutions of this sort received recognition from the National Educational Association as a Department of Business Education in 1894.[68] The Columbian Exposition at Chicago serves as a date for them as well as did the one at Philadelphia for trade schools. Since institutions of the former sort had many shortcomings, powerful business voices in the nineties joined in the demand for domestication in high schools of the commercial course. The American Bankers' Association took up the matter largely as an appendage to business schools at the college level,[69] and the New York Chamber of Commerce resolved that "it favors the establishment and development of sounder commercial education, both in secondary schools and higher institutions of learning." [70] Demands of this sort rose

[67] *Ibid.*, pp. 467–470; S. S. Packard, "The Evolution of Business Colleges," *Proceedings of the International Congress of Education . . . 1893*, pp. 789–790.

[68] R. F. Gallagher, "President's Address," *N.E.A. Proceedings, 1894*, pp. 961–963.

[69] E. J. James, *A Plea for the Establishment of Commercial High Schools. An Address before the Convention of the American Bankers' Association . . . 1892* (New York: American Bankers' Association, 1893), pp. 10–11.

[70] *Forty-first Annual Report of the Corporation of the Chamber of Commerce of the State of New-York for the Year 1898–'99*, I, 33–35.

from puissant individuals in business and education,[71] and from "the young, vigorous American business-man, who is not so far removed from his schooling in the secondary school as to have forgotten what it failed to give him." [72]

Such acceptability as trade or commercial education secured was attended with some blurring of the logic of the case in their behalf. It was discovered that both of these new subject matters were "cultural" and moral. Manual training was "the coeducation of all the senses."

Each educational brick used in the grand structure of moral and mental development should be laid in a trowelful of common-sense, manual training cement, to bind together every particle from foundation to weathercock into a harmonious, well-rounded, beautiful tower of strength, fitted and able to withstand the blasts of social and political storms that sooner or later must assail it.[73]

As for business training, it had "higher aspects." Stenography was "a profession," bookkeeping a matter of ethics. Of course these subjects trained character, mind, and morals. Business education "will, by appealing to the lower motives of securing business prosperity thru

[71] E. R. Johnson, "Business Education in the High Schools," *N.E.A. Proceedings, 1898*, p. 870.

[72] W. C. Stevenson, "The Advent of the Commercial High School," *N.E.A. Proceedings, 1899*, p. 1026.

[73] Paul Hoffman, "Manual Training in New York City Schools," *N.E.A. Proceedings, 1892*, p. 472; *Forty-first Annual Report of the Corporation of the Chamber of Commerce of the State of New-York . . . 1898–'99*, I, 39.

economy, thrift, and health, do more to root out tobacco using, gambling, idleness, and spendthrift habits than all your preaching, however eloquent." [74]

These and cognate developments, Robert H. Thurston, once president of Stevens Institute and later head of Sibley College, Cornell University, surveyed with characteristic acumen at the International Congress of Education, held at the Chicago Columbian Exposition in 1893. His picture was not only of things actual but also of things desirable.

For people of wealth, twenty years of culture, five of professional study, may be none too extensive a course; but the citizen of moderate means must at least terminate his son's studies at twenty-one, and if he is to have a professional training, it must commence at sixteen or seventeen; while the so-called "industrial classes" must send their offspring out into the world to earn their own living while still children. It thus happens that the education of the people must, in the main, be such as will give them technological training, with, incidentally, so much of culture as can be offered without detriment to their preparation for the work that must probably be theirs for life. We have here the reason at once for a complete and perfect system

[74] Stevenson, *op. cit.*, pp. 1029–1030; R. F. Gallagher, "The Higher Aspects of Business Education," and I. S. Dement, "Stenography and Typewriting as Branches of Business Education," *Proceedings of the International Congress of Education . . . 1893*, pp. 796–800; A. S. Osborn, "The Disciplinary Value of the Business Course," *N.E.A. Proceedings, 1894*, pp. 989–994; E. J. James, "The Commercial High School as Part of Secondary Education," *School Review*, II (1894), 577–579.

of education by the state, and for the organization of special manual-training, trade, and professional schools.[75]

Such a scheme of things, however much in touch with economic realities, certainly ran counter to the deeply cherished democratic faith of American education that any child, no matter what his origin, could grow to the highest culture.[76] Perhaps the scheme of education desired by the business community was at the bottom anti-democratic.

Though many factors shaped their decisions, it must be remembered that the people were constantly voting on the existing educational structure by withdrawing their children from or not sending them to school. Even the Committee of Ten stopped pontificating long enough to remark that only an "insignificant percentage" of high school graduates continued to college; the higher proportion of girls than of boys in high school also showed a dissatisfaction with the curriculum as unsuited to the latter's needs.[77] In the end the businessman's cam-

[75] R. H. Thurston, "Technological Schools: Their Purpose and Its Accomplishment," *Proceedings of the International Congress of Education* . . . *1893*, pp. 535–536, 538–539.

[76] C. M. Woodward, "What Should Be Added to the Essential Branches of the Elementary Course of Study to Meet the Industrial Needs of the Localities?" *Proceedings of the International Congress of Education* . . . *1893*, pp. 266–268.

[77] "Report of the Committee of Ten," p. 1444; J. L. Snyder, "Education for the Industrial Classes," *N.E.A. Proceedings, 1898*, pp. 760–763; D. W. Springer, "Business Education," *ibid.*, p. 860; *Report of the Committee* [on Education and Labor] *of the Senate* . . . *1885*, III, 500.

paign for education for use was also a people's crusade.[78]

[78] H. M. Leipziger, "The Progress of Manual Training," *N.E.A. Proceedings, 1894,* pp. 877–879; W. J. Amos, "An Ideal Business College," *ibid.,* pp. 971–972; Johnson, *op. cit.,* pp. 867–868; E. J. James, "The Commercial High School," pp. 583–584.

IV

"The Higher Learning"

LET us begin with certain statistics which are a matter
of record. Following the Civil War, men of wealth
greatly increased their donations to higher education.
Whereas before that conflict Abbott Lawrence's gift
of $50,000 to Harvard had been of exceptional size for
an institution at the college level, a merchant-banker,
Johns Hopkins, gave by will in 1870 $3,500,000 to
found a university in Baltimore; Leland Stanford gave
$24,000,000 to a university named after his son and
located on the family farm in California; and John D.
Rockefeller, under astute guidance, contributed all in
all $34,000,000 to rescue the University of Chicago

from obscurity and transform it into a great university. Officially he became "the Founder." [1] As far as our time period is concerned, the great foundations which did so much for education were just over the horizon. Hand in hand with the dollar, the businessman marched into the potential control room of Academe. Whereas clergymen had once dominated boards of trustees, businessmen, bankers, and lawyers now took their place. Working with a very limited sample of fifteen private institutions of higher learning, Earl J. McGrath, later to become Commissioner of Education of the United States, found that from 1860–1861 to 1900–1901 the percentage of businessmen on boards increased from 22.8 to 25.7; of bankers from 4.6 to 12.8; and of lawyers from 20.6 to 25.7. Perhaps to redress this picture it should be added that the percentage of educators was at the same time increasing from 5 to 8.[2]

Conceivably this business interest in higher education might be, as Veblen in his essay on *The Theory of the Leisure Class* implied, another evidence of the rich seeking for merely honorific associations. Or it might be a response such as Abram Hewitt, steel master, son-in-law of Peter Cooper, and graduate of Columbia, expressed in dedicating the new Morningside Heights campus of

[1] Richard Hofstadter and W. P. Metzger, *The Development of Academic Freedom in the United States* (New York: Columbia University Press, 1955), p. 413.

[2] E. J. McGrath, "The Control of Higher Education in America," *Educational Record*, XVII (April, 1936), 263–265.

that institution in 1896: "In this country patents of no-
bility are wisely prohibited, but a title to immortality
is surely within the reach of those to whom the trustees
may finally award the privilege and the glory of erecting
any one of these buildings." [3] This appeal was honorific,
too.

Occasionally prominent businessmen uttered crav-
ings for learning. Commodore Vanderbilt, the consum-
mate Philistine in matters of taste, once incautiously
confessed to the clergyman his wife had introduced into
the family to give a higher direction to her husband's
interests, "I'd give a million dollars to-day, Doctor, if
I had your education!" Somewhat startled by the family
surprise at this heretical utterance, the Commodore
backtracked a little: "I seem to get along better than half
of your educated men." [4] More representative in all
probability were the opinions of Andrew Carnegie.
Granting that the old academic training was a necessary
prelude for the learned professions, Carnegie regarded
the latter with measured enthusiasm. True, these sought
from life fame rather than the more "ignoble" materialism of wealth, but all through the professions—politics,
law, and religion—there was a flaw, a "narrow, selfish,
personal vanity." On whether the education given in an

[3] A. S. Hewitt, "Liberty, Learning, and Property," in Allan
Nevins, ed., *Selected Writings of Abram S. Hewitt* (New York:
Columbia University Press, 1937), pp. 334–335.
[4] W. A. Croffut, *The Vanderbilts and the Story of Their Fortune* (Chicago and New York: Belford, Clarke, 1886), pp. 137–138.

"academic" or "literary" college was desirable for those going into business, Carnegie weighed no alternatives.

Men have wasted their precious years, trying to extract education from an ignorant past whose chief province is to teach us, not what to adopt, but what to avoid. Men have sent their sons to colleges to waste their energies upon obtaining a knowledge of such languages as Greek and Latin, which are of no more practical use to them than Choctaw. . . . They have been crammed with the details of petty and insignificant skirmishes between savages, and taught to exalt a band of ruffians into heroes; and we have called them "educated." They have been "educated" as if they were destined for life upon some other planet than this. . . . What they have obtained has served to imbue them with false ideas and to give them a distaste for practical life. . . . Had they gone into active work during the years spent at college they would have been better educated men in every true sense of that term. The fire and energy have been stamped out of them, and how to so manage as to live a life of idleness and not a life of usefulness has become the chief question with them.

Except for those who had "antiquarian" tastes and for those going into the professions, "the education given today in our colleges is a positive disadvantage." [5]

[5] Andrew Carnegie, *The Empire of Business* (New York: Doubleday, 1902), pp. 79–81, 145–147; *Report of the Committee* [on Education and Labor] *of the Senate upon the Relations between Labor and Capital, 1885*, II, 1099; Joseph Wharton, *Is a College Education Advantageous to a Business Man? Address Delivered by Joseph Wharton at the Reception Given February*

Judgments such as these were echoed by other than businessmen. A labor agitator from the mid-West announced: "We have no objection to the education of rich men's sons—too proud to work and too lazy to steal—at private schools and colleges, to become lawyers, doctors, preachers or what not." [6] And Henry George, counseling his namesake son on whether he should go to Harvard or the Brooklyn *Eagle,* concluded, "Going to college, you will make life friendships but you will come out filled with much that will have to be unlearned. Going to newspaper work, you will come in touch with the practical world, will be getting a profession and learning to make yourself useful." [7] In sum, from the business point of view the indictment against the American college was that it delayed the start in business life, taught what was useless, and gave students bad habits and bad attitudes, the worst of which was a desire to live by wit rather than work and a disbelief in the dignity of labor.[8] Those with these fears were hardly reassured by two articles in the *North American*

20th, 1890, by the Wharton School Association [n.p., n.d.], pp. 1–14.

[6] *Report of the Committee* [on Education and Labor] *of the Senate . . . 1885,* II, 1383.

[7] C. A. Barker, *Henry George* (New York: Oxford, 1955), p. 339.

[8] C. H. Thurber, "Is the Present High School Course a Satisfactory Preparation for Business? If Not, How Should It Be Modified?" *N.E.A. Proceedings, 1897* (Chicago: University of Chicago Press, 1897), pp. 809–810; *Report of the Committee* [on Education and Labor] *of the Senate . . . 1885,* II, 964, 1203; III, 296.

Review of 1888: "The Fast Set at Harvard University" and a rejoinder to it almost as disturbing as the original indictment.[9]

If this disfavor for college education is coupled with the flood of donations and the infiltration of college directorates by businessmen, a natural inference would be that business had a systematic, concrete transformation which it wished to effect throughout higher education. Of its paper power on the premises there was little doubt. Charters and laws gave to presidents and trustees embracing authority in matters general and detailed. One trustee of Northwestern University, a patent lawyer and an officer of the Western Railroad Association, declared,

As to what should be taught in political and social science they [the professors] should promptly and gracefully submit to the determination of the trustees when the latter find it necessary to act. . . . If the trustees err it is for the patrons and proprietors, not for the employees, to change either the policy or the personnel of the board.[10]

When an outsider polled some trustees at Chicago, Columbia, Princeton, Yale, Johns Hopkins, Pennsylvania, and American University, he found that their opinion agreed almost unanimously with the oracle from North-

[9] Aleck Quest, "The Fast Set at Harvard University," *North American Review*, CXLVII (Nov., 1888), 542–553; " 'The Fast Set' at Harvard," *North American Review*, CXLVII (Dec., 1888), 643–653.

[10] Quoted in Hofstadter and Metzger, *op. cit.*, p. 459.

western.[11] But it was one thing to assert a power and another to exercise it. In actuality the revolution which business desired was not brought about at the guillotine. In 1930 Arthur O. Lovejoy, one of the founders of the American Association of University Professors and one of the earliest and doughtiest champions of academic freedom, could write in the *Encyclopedia of the Social Sciences:* "The greater gifts to American education have, however, usually been notably exempt from formal restrictions upon freedom of teaching; and in a number of privately endowed universities, it [academic freedom] has been better assured than in many state institutions." [12] That more heads did not roll was partly due to the fact that the guild of scholars and teachers was in general conservative and had mastered the adroit arts of compromise, postponement, and evasive action.[13]

The easiest way for innovators, therefore, was to start *de novo,*—to establish a new institution with new purposes, and if possible a new faculty, recruited from academic progressives. A clear need for a nation dependent upon steam, electricity, and invention was technical or engineering instruction. "Every college," asserted

[11] G. H. Shibley, "The University and Social Questions," *Arena,* XXIII (March, 1900), 296.

[12] "Academic Freedom," *Encyclopedia of the Social Sciences,* I, 387.

[13] C. F. Adams, Jr., *A College Fetich. An Address Delivered Before the Harvard Chapter of the Fraternity of the Phi Beta Kappa, in Sanders Theatre, Cambridge, June 28, 1883* (Boston: Lee and Shepard, 1884), p. 9.

Joseph Medill of the Chicago *Tribune*, "should have a department of mechanism and a chemical laboratory to impart the secrets of nature and the sources of force." [14] Existing colleges sought to adjust to such demands and new institutions came into existence to meet them. The obligation to create and finance these experiments was at the outset, as so many addresses put it, one for private philanthropy. Well before the Civil War, at Harvard and at Yale foresighted administrators or devoted teachers had undertaken instruction in science applied to arts and industries. Usually no funds were available. But in 1847 Abbott Lawrence, merchant, manufacturer, and railroad builder, made the first of his donations to the Harvard enterprise. The Lawrence Scientific School was intended to be an engineering one. A decade later, Joseph E. Sheffield of New Haven, promoter, financier, and builder of railroads in the mid-West and in New England, took pity on the struggling efforts of Yale to provide instruction in applied science and gave a building and an endowment to the Sheffield Scientific School. [15]

Like so many things in Boston, the Massachusetts Institute of Technology was a compound of business

[14] *Report of the Committee* [on Education and Labor] *of the Senate . . . 1885*, II, 964.

[15] S. E. Morison, ed., *The Development of Harvard University Since the Inauguration of President Eliot, 1869–1929* (Cambridge: Harvard University Press, 1930), pp. 412–415; R. H. Chittenden, *History of the Sheffield Scientific School of Yale University, 1846–1922* (New Haven: Yale University Press, 1928), I, 37–74; II, 586–587.

enterprise and vaulting culture. Taking advantage of the fact that the state was filling in the Back Bay, a region which eventually became Boston's "West End," William B. Rogers, a Virginia-born scientist, and others conceived of asking the state for a land grant in that area on which to construct a civic cultural center. The Massachusetts Institute of Technology was a covering term for a Society of the Arts, to be devoted to research and publication, for a museum for the Boston Society of Natural History, and for a School of Industrial Science. Although the petitioners asserted that "in the recent progress of the Industrial Arts, including commerce and agriculture, as well as the manufacturing and more strictly, mechanical pursuits—we meet with daily-increasing proofs of the happy influence of scientific culture on the industry and the civilization of nations," and although they enlisted among their sponsors the Boston Board of Trade,[16] the Legislature was unfavorably impressed by the amorphous character of their proposals. Eventually, however, the General Court gave a grant

[16] *Objects and Plan of an Institute of Technology. Including a Society of Arts, A Museum of Arts, and a School of Industrial Science. Proposed to Be Established in Boston* (Boston: John Wilson and Son, 1860); *An Account of the Proceedings Preliminary to the Organization of the Massachusetts Institute of Technology, with a List of Members Thus Far Associated and an Appendix and Resolutions in Aid of the Objects of the Committee of Associated Institutions of Science and Art* (Boston: John Wilson and Son, 1861); *Scope and Plan of the School of Industrial Science of the Massachusetts Institute of Technology, as Reported by the Committee of Instruction of the Institute, and Adopted by the Government, May 30, 1864* (Boston: John Wilson and Son, 1864).

of lands on condition the promoters raise $100,000. The largest of the donations discharging this stipulation came from Doctor William J. Walker of Charlestown, Massachusetts, who had retired from medicine to accumulate a fortune in railroad and manufacturing stocks in order that he "could contribute to education." On his death his millions were distributed to his family and forty feminine friends and to three educational institutions. Harvard had earlier refused a gift to the Medical School because this most piquant of donors, cannily aware of the prerequisites to innovation, had insisted upon a faculty acceptable to him.[17] The Massachusetts General Court also came to the rescue by assigning a portion of the national land grant under the Morrill Act to the Institute as a College of Mechanic Arts.[18] This good luck apparently gave more urgency to the proposal for an industrial and practical institution. Edward Atkinson, cotton capitalist and member of the Board of Government of the Institute, confessed years later that he and his associates "were qualified . . . to direct that institution by what we did not know more than by what we did." [19] Nor did they have the only word in the matter. William Atkinson, brother of Edward and a

[17] "William Johnson Walker," *Dictionary of American Biography*, XIX, 366.

[18] *Life and Letters of William Barton Rogers*, ed. by his wife (Boston and New York: Houghton, 1896), II, 107–109, 143–145, 155, 163–164.

[19] E. J. James, *An Address before the Convention of the American Bankers' Association at Saratoga, September 3, 1890* (New York: American Bankers' Association, 1892), p. 38.

professor at the Institute, was writing in 1866, a year after the school was opened, that the faculty were debating whether Tech should be limited to the special sciences taught "with a modicum" of English, French, and German, or whether through a curriculum of English and scientific courses Tech should replace the classical one of older institutions, but still "aim as they do, to give a well-proportioned liberal education." [20]

Among the most persistent correspondents of Francis Amasa Walker, the second president of the Institute and its real founder, was Governor Leland Stanford who, seeking for some therapy to lift the grief of himself and his wife over the death of an idolized son, had determined to found at Palo Alto a university for the children of California. Despite the myriad consultants to whom he applied, Stanford had an accurate idea of the kind of institution he wanted. Ordinarily reserved, on this matter he talked freely:

I have been impressed with the fact that of all the young men who come to me with letters of introduction from friends in the East, the most helpless class are college men. . . . They are generally prepossessing in appearance and of good stock, but when they seek employment, and I ask them what they can do, all they can say is "anything." They have no definite technical knowledge of anything. They have no specific aim, no definite purpose. It is to overcome that condition, to give an education which shall not have that result, which I hope will be the aim of this Univer-

[20] Letter to Edward Atkinson, January 18, 1866, Atkinson Papers, M.H.S.

sity. . . . Its capacity to give a practical not a theoretical education ought to be accordingly foremost.[21]

Of the first ten appointments to the Faculty made and accepted, there were only two not in engineering and science; of these exceptions one was a college administrator and another, Andrew D. White, "Non-Resident Professor of History." [22]

For many schools other than M.I.T., the Morrill Act of 1862, the charter of the land-grant colleges, provided stimulus and means. There is no need for me to reemphasize how its receipt in New York State enabled Ezra Cornell and Andrew D. White to establish Cornell University with its motto—"I would found an institution where any person can find instruction in any study," including science and engineering.[23] So much attention has been directed to the Morrill Act in terms of the type of institution that developed, the "people's colleges," that not enough emphasis has yet been directed to the background of the act, aside from the agricultural influence. Not surprisingly in view of his location in an industrial state, President Wayland of Brown University seems to have been an early expositor of the advantages of industrial education, in the narrow sense of that term; Justin Morrill, the Vermont Representative whose name the act honored, also admitted that "as

[21] O. L. Elliott, *Stanford University: The First Twenty-Five Years* (Stanford: Stanford University Press, 1937), pp. 19–20.

[22] *Ibid.*, pp. 23, 24, 55.

[23] A. D. White, *Autobiography of Andrew Dickson White* (New York: Century, 1922), I, 300.

the son of a hard-headed blacksmith," he "could not overlook mechanics." [24] Perhaps one explanation for the neglect of this phase of the Morrill Act is that, as President Francis Amasa Walker said later, the "exigency" for the Morrill Act was not "very great." [25] Certainly after it, as before, men of business continued to found and support schools of applied science and of engineering. It would be a mistake, however, to feel that wealthy men were the only founders. As Walker said of schools of technology, "They were created through the foresight, the unselfish devotion, the strenuous endeavors of a few rich men, and of very many poor men, known as professors of mathematics, chemistry, physics, and geology." [26]

Obviously enheartened by their success with schools of technology and engineering, some business leaders began to consider the possibility of establishing colleges for instruction in business, institutions of more repute and higher standards than the proprietary "business colleges" of the day. Some businessmen were, to be sure, given pause as to what such institutions of higher business learning should teach—an enduring problem.

[24] E. D. Ross, *Democracy's College: The Land-Grant Movement in the Formative Stage* (Ames, Iowa: Iowa State College Press, 1942), pp. 15, 16, 48–52.

[25] *Report of the Committee* [on Education and Labor] *of the Senate . . . 1885*, III, 331.

[26] R. H. Thurston, "Technological Schools: Their Purpose and Its Accomplishment," *Proceedings of the International Congress of Education . . . 1893* (New York: National Educational Association, 1894), p. 546.

Charles Elliott Perkins in the nineties wrote Henry L. Higginson, the Boston banker,

You might teach hotel keeping at Cambridge, but you can't teach railroading, because it involves too much. You can teach branches of it, as you do now—engineering and drawing, for example. But the commercial part of it—how to save part of every dollar you get in and how to get in all you can—that you cannot teach at school.[27]

Yet already a Philadelphia merchant, Joseph Wharton, had submitted a plan to the trustees of the University of Pennsylvania and accompanied it with a gift of $100,000. In 1881 the Wharton School of Finance and Economy was opened. The motives were in part honorific—Wharton wished to commemorate a "family name which has been honorably borne in this community since the foundation of the city"—but in greater part educational. Wharton was particularly impressed by the plight of young men who inherited wealth. Since they could not be reclaimed by hard work, as their fathers had been, higher education of the right sort was the answer. We aim to produce "educated young men with a taste for business, vigorous, active workers, of sturdy character and independent opinion, having a lofty faith in all things good, and able to give a reason for the faith that is in them." The proposed course of instruction was superior to the apprenticeship in business which Carnegie was to celebrate; apprenticeship resulted

[27] 1895(?), Perkins Private Letters and Memos, R.C.O.

in narrowness and empiricism, nor was it systematic.[28] Among the five professorships Wharton foresaw for his school, only two seemed strictly vocational— the professorship of accounting and that of mercantile law. The others—professors on money, banking, industry, commerce, and transportation—were clearly to provide a "liberal education in all matters concerning Finance and Commerce."

This was liberal in the sense of general, for the donor specified in formidable detail what was to be taught. The professor of money and currency was to teach "particularly the necessity of permanent uniformity or integrity in the coin unit upon which the money system of a nation is based" and "the advantages of an adequate precious-metal fund for settling international balances as well as for regulating and checking by redemption the paper money and credits of a modern nation." For his part, the Professor on Industry, Commerce, and Transportation should demonstrate

how a great nation should be as far as possible self-sufficient, maintaining a proper balance between agriculture, mining, and manufactures, and supplying its own wants; how mutual advantage results from reciprocal exchange of commodities natural to one land for the diverse commodities natural to another, but how by craft in commerce one nation may take the substance of a rival and maintain for itself a virtual monopoly of the most profitable and civilizing industries; how by suitable tariff legislation a nation

[28] James, *op. cit.*, pp. 10–19, 23, 30.

may thwart such designs, may keep its productive industry active, cheapen the cost of commodities, and oblige foreigners to sell to it at low prices while contributing largely toward defraying the expenses of its government.[29]

The gospel of protection appears again as one among several items prescribed in a section entitled "general tendency of instruction." [30] The curriculum drawn up under these injunctions included philosophy, a course in the history of relations between church and state, and heavy doses of government and history, the latter with a list toward the social and economic.[31] Probably the Wharton School was in the light of modern educational practice largely a device to give students at the University of Pennsylvania a major in history and the social sciences.

Probably the fact the school did not lead directly to a career, along with its reputed easiness, was the reason it was only "moderately successful" and that "the most vigorous young men went elsewhere." [32] At least these were the admissions of William H. Rhawn, a Philadelphia banker, who toward the end of the eighties, began a campaign to put the American Bankers' Association behind the idea of improved business instruction. His apostle for the new gospel was Edmund J. James, Professor of Public Finance and Administration

---

[29] *Ibid.*, p. 31.   [30] *Ibid.*, p. 34.

[31] *Ibid.*, pp. 23–24; E. F. Goldman, *John Bach McMaster, American Historian* (Philadelphia: University of Pennsylvania Press, 1943), pp. 51–52.

[32] James, *op. cit.*, pp. 27–28.

in the Wharton School. James delivered a series of papers before the bankers and elsewhere and talked and organized personally to such good purpose that he became president in turn of Northwestern University and of the University of Illinois.[33] Meanwhile Rhawn secured from the American Bankers' Association a resolution "most earnestly" commending "not only to bankers but to all intelligent and progressive citizens throughout our country the founding of schools of finance and economy for the business training of our children, to be established in connection with the universities and colleges of the land upon . . . the Wharton plan." [34]

Actually all this exhortation and exertion resulted up to the new century in the establishment of only two such institutions—one at the University of California and a second at the University of Chicago. At the former institution a committee of the Regents was wildly enthusiastic over a school which met the "demands of practical men," made "successful business men," and "kept them at their career." The California situation was unique. The state was isolated, and since its production was "far beyond the consumption of our people" new markets must be developed, particularly "in the Pacific Ocean which invites us to the greatest commercial conquest of all times." A School of Commerce was a means to this end.[35] At the University of Chicago, where all

---

[33] "Edmund Janes James," *Dictionary of American Biography*, IX, 574–575.

[34] James, *op. cit.*, p. 37.

[35] *Annual Report of the Secretary to the Board of Regents of*

things were new, the administration made haste slowly because of "the desire of the authorities being not to lay too great emphasis upon work of this character, in contrast with the longer-established college work, in the early years of the University." [36]

Here as elsewhere, failure is sometimes more revealing than success. In the late nineties the Chamber of Commerce of the State of New York entered into negotiations with Seth Low, one of its members who was also President of Columbia University, about the establishment at the University of a course in commercial history, commercial geography, domestic and foreign commercial law, and accounting, which the Chamber would finance with $10,000.[37] Years later announcing the establishment of a business school, Professor E. R. A. Seligman of the Department of Economics revealed how the academicians had successfully blighted this early courtship. Anyone who has listened to faculty discussions can hear the familiar overtones: students of quality and a faculty of competence could not be recruited, and more importantly the "Department of Economics and others realized the real obligation was graduate work and research rather than professional

---

the University of California for the Year Ending June 30, 1898 (Berkeley: University of California Press, 1898), pp. 34–38.

[36] W. R. Harper, *The President's Report: Administration, Decennial Publications* (Chicago: University of Chicago Press, 1903), I, lxxxix–xci.

[37] *Forty-first Annual Report of the Corporation of the Chamber of Commerce of the State of New York for the Year 1898-'99,* pp. xiv, xx, 34.

teaching." The best policy was "wait and see." [38] Business meanwhile had to find such comfort as it could in the School of Political Science with its general and philosophical studies.[39]

Actually, of course the establishment of technological and business schools with concrete practical programs was not the nub of the matter. The real issue was the transformation, if any, that the vision and demands of businessmen wrought in the literary colleges and their traditional curriculum. That the business community should continue to display an interest in higher learning of this sort certainly challenges explanation. As will be revealed later, Veblen's theory that the leisure class in a pecuniary culture wanted this higher learning precisely because it was useless does not square with what was going on. Businessmen did not want to sacrifice their sons to any Deity "sicklied o'er with the pale cast of thought." [40] One businessman father rejoiced that his son had failed the examinations for the College of the City of New York and had thus been saved from a life of "elegant leisure." "Whenever I find a rich man dying and leaving a large amount of money to found a college, I say to myself, 'It is a pity he had not died while he was poor.' " [41]

[38] E. R. A. Seligman, "A University School of Business," *Columbia University Quarterly*, XVIII (June, 1916), 242.

[39] Hewitt, *op. cit.*, p. 333.

[40] But see *Proceedings of the International Congress of Education . . . 1893*, p. 551.

[41] *Report of the Committee* [on Education and Labor] *of the Senate . . . 1885*, II, 1114–1118.

Still it might be argued that the refinements, resulting from a classical education, had a practical value. Commodore Vanderbilt's unexpected allegiance to the life of the mind was the voice of experience: "I've been to England, and seen them lords, and other fellows, and knew that I had twice as much brains as they had maybe, and yet I had to keep still, and couldn't say anything through fear of exposing myself." [42] Once when James Caldwell, Tennessee utilities magnate and banker, came North to see Morgan "on a matter of business," he had to wait while the "superintendent of the Art Museum of New York" and the banker opened and examined

a treasure which had just arrived from Europe. It proved to be a plain-looking picture, executed upon a board, and called the "Fra Angelica." It clearly was antique, and no doubt a very rare piece, but not pretty, and to me, who am no art critic, it seemed quite ordinary; but he and the art superintendent took on over it mightily and it was quite some time before we could get him back to "business." [43]

Clearly something more than accounting or commercial law was required to impress a banker who preferred to deal with "gentlemen" who could be invited on board his yacht and into his library.[44]

Though some sacrifice was probably desirable in order to be at ease with contacts, the interest of busi-

[42] Croffut, *op. cit.*, p. 137.

[43] J. E. Caldwell, *Recollections of a Life Time* (Nashville, Tenn.: Baird-Ward Press, 1923), p. 235.

[44] F. L. Allen, *The Great Pierpont Morgan* (New York: Harper, 1949), pp. 96–97.

nessmen in literary education was usually remote from calculations of loss and gain. Higher education simply was "a good thing," and they wished to finance it; let able educators determine the detailed objectives of expenditures. Of Johns Hopkins, Daniel Coit Gilman, first president of the Baltimore Göttingen, wrote, "Fortunately, the founder . . . did not define the distinguished name that he bestowed upon his child, nor embarrass its future by needless conditions. Details were left to a sagacious board of trustees whom he charged with the duty of supervision." [45] In the nineties Rockefeller's ideas on higher education were probably somewhat similar, though it is hard to disentangle them from the opinions of the swarms of solicitors and counselors buzzing around him. The University of Chicago, the destination of his great benefaction, was to "*help the world*" and "to do the world more good." The implementation of these vague and lofty purposes, what the age knew as "uplift," was left to "the management." [46] On those rare, celebrant occasions when the oil king was tempted to the Midway campus and cajoled into giving speech, he explained his philanthropy to the institution on the grounds of Christian stewardship and advised students that some must be followers and fill the "humblest positions uncomplainingly and acceptably." Find your

[45] D. C. Gilman, *The Launching of a University and Other Papers, A Sheaf of Remembrances* (New York: Dodd, 1906), p. 7.
[46] Allan Nevins, ed., *Study in Power: John D. Rockefeller, Industrialist and Philanthropist* (New York: Scribner, 1953), II, 182, 185, 190.

niche. "Whatever position this is, it is the highest position in the sight of good men and in the economy of God." Certainly this is one of the few echoes at the college level of the argument heard for lower education that it served the safety of the *status quo*. Even here the connection is inferential.[47]

Most businessmen did not resort to Christian and Platonic generalization to justify the changes they wanted in higher education. In their eyes, the greatest waste of time in college was the very core of the curriculum—the classics. In spite of Senator Pugh of Alabama, who felt Latin and Greek disqualified students "from all industrial pursuits," [48] there were distinctions between the languages. In 1897 among the businessmen of Chicago polled by Professor Thurber, no one believed Greek had "any practical value," one thought that for those employed in business law, collections and credits, or in executive departments handling correspondence, Latin was "highly advantageous," though salesmen and buyers did not need it.[49] Over a decade earlier Charles Francis Adams, Jr., president of the Union Pacific, speaking in the consecrated spaces of Sanders Theatre, informed the Harvard Phi Beta Kappa that the worship of Latin and Greek was a college fetich.

[47] Harper, *op. cit.*, I, xli; Hewitt, *op. cit.*, p. 336.

[48] *Report of the Committee* [on Education and Labor] *of the Senate . . . 1885*, III, 160.

[49] C. H. Thurber, "Is the Present High School Course a Satisfactory Preparation for Business? If Not, How Should It Be Modified?" *N.E.A. Proceedings, 1897* (Chicago: University of Chicago Press, 1897), p. 811.

Latin I will not stop to contend over. That is a small matter. Not only is it a comparatively simple language, . . . but it has its modern uses. Not only is it directly the mother tongue of all southwestern Europe, but it has by common consent been adopted in scientific nomenclature. Hence, there are reasons why the educated man should have at least an elementary knowledge of Latin. . . . The study of Greek—as a traditional requirement—is a positive educational wrong. It has already wrought great individual and general injury, and is now working it. It has been productive of no compensating advantage. It is a superstition.[50]

What to put in their place? French and German, "working tools" of the modern age, perchance even Spanish. "There is a saying that a living dog is better than a dead lion; and the Spanish tongue is what the Greek is not,— a very considerable American fact." [51] James Caldwell, who could not afford to be as bold as an Adams because he was not as cultured, thought the classics should be studied first in translation: "By the way, I think Dryden's translation of the Aeneid is as remarkable and shows as much talent as Vergil did in the original." [52] Unwittingly, L. C. Armstrong, the masterful principal of Hampton Institute, put the antithesis in a nut shell: "The darkey," he wrote, "prefers Greek to common sense—like everybody else." [53] Veblen to the contrary

[50] *Op. cit.,* pp. 16–17.

[51] *Ibid.,* p. 35; Wharton, *op. cit.,* pp. 16–17.

[52] *Op. cit.,* p. 267.

[53] Letter to Edward Atkinson, Jan. 23, 1880, Atkinson Papers, M.H.S.

notwithstanding,[54] the business banner read, "Greek must go." And it did, first as a requirement for admission, then for the degree of A.B. This successful outcome, it should be pointed out, owed quite as much to college administrators, like Eliot of Harvard and Hyde of Bowdoin, as to businessmen inside or outside of boards of trustees.[55]

One motive for the drive against Greek was the desire to find room for something else. Curriculum builders and tinkerers always come up against the hard fact that four years have only so much time. The business community, which, as we have seen earlier, was relying upon political economy and even developing the discipline's resources, might have been expected to approve the insertion into the curriculum of more instruction in this and related subjects. Unhappily for the academic prosperity of these subject matters, businessmen feared them as foes or sought them as allies to their prejudices. Thus an independent oil operator anticipated if students would devote themselves to social science rather than "pouring over musty dead languages, learning the disgusting stories of the mythical gods, and all the barbarous stuff of the dead past, . . . then a Standard Oil Company would be impossible." [56] Others dreaded, and quite

[54] Thorstein Veblen, *The Theory of the Leisure Class: An Economic Study of Institutions* (New York: Macmillan, 1908), p. 382.

[55] Henry James, *Charles W. Eliot: President of Harvard University, 1869–1909* (Boston: Houghton, 1930), I, 366–367; L. C. Hatch, *The History of Bowdoin College* (Portland, Maine: Loring, Short & Harmon, 1927), pp. 186–188.

[56] *Report of the Committee* [on Education and Labor] *of the Senate . . . 1885*, II, 1099.

rightly, that free-trade textbooks would be used.[57] With his customary acumen, Charles Elliott Perkins penetrated to a deeper, troubling question.

My idea of teaching is that you have got to *know* something before you begin, & that it is for that reason that the world has settled down into a belief that the classics are the best studies for training the mind. . . . No two doctors would agree about what is called political economy, of which the late Francis Walker, and, say, Professor Perry may be taken as distinguished teachers, & yet diametrically opposed to one another on the most important question political economy deals with, and that is the question of money and its influence on the affairs of mankind.[58]

President Andrew D. White exhibited his usual guilefulness as an administrator when he established instruction in economics at Cornell. He had lecturers on both sides of contested opinions. Even then "sundry good people" complained "it was like calling a professor of atheism into a theological seminary." [59]

However much curriculum changes undermined the business indictment that college learning was useless, they were a minor factor in overcoming the assertion that colleges inculcated wrong attitudes and habits. What was really important was a change in the morals and tone of these institutions. This was not a matter of compulsory chapel. As far as one can see, when chapel went under, as it sometimes did, business-minded trus-

[57] Thurber, *op. cit.*, p. 813.

[58] Letter to F. A. Delano, 1895(?), Perkins Private Letters and Memos, R.C.O.

[59] White, *op. cit.*, I, 380–381.

tees or alumni hardly murmured. Furthermore in the technical schools the requirement of compulsory chapel attendance was waived, perchance on the ground that the scientific course was ill adapted to the saving of souls.[60] Yet it was these very schools that led the way to a new dispensation in morals and habits. Francis Amasa Walker, surveying the possibilities of the affiliation of M.I.T. with a university, concluded that the advantages would be dearly bought

if the technical students, through association with a university, are to come habitually in contact with young men who have not seriously taken up the work of their lives, who regard college merely as a place in which to have a good time or to indulge in sport or dissipation, who have no settled purpose and no manly aims, and especially if the technical students are to come habitually in contact with young men who regard labor as degrading, who look upon the rough clothes and the stained fingers of the laboratory and the workshop as badges of inferiority in character or in social standing.[61]

[60] L. B. Richardson, *History of Dartmouth College* (Hanover, N.H.: Dartmouth College Publications, 1932), II, 625; White, *op. cit.*, I, 402–406; Henry James, *op. cit.*, I, 380–382; S. E. Morison, *Three Centuries of Harvard* (Cambridge: Harvard University Press, 1936), p. 360; F. G. Peabody, "Voluntary Worship, 1886–1929," in S. E. Morison, ed., *The Development of Harvard University* . . . , pp. li–liv; G. W. Pierson, *Yale College: An Educational History, 1871–1921* (New Haven: Yale University Press, 1952), pp. 12–14.

[61] "Opening Address of the Chairman," *Proceedings of the International Congress of Education* . . . *1893*, pp. 531–532.

And the Boston *Herald* saluted M.I.T. as a place without "the fast habits, hazing, lawless behavior, foppery and frivolity which are so often associated with college life." It was a place of work and self-help.[62] That institutions of a different sort should strive for a similar tone was evident from Joseph Wharton's meticulous instructions for his school: "The students must be taught and drilled, not lectured to without care whether or not attention is paid; any lazy or incompetent student must be dismissed." [63] Nor were donors the only ones pushing higher education in the direction of "hardness." Faculty, flowing back from the German universities, introduced new standards of performance and individual responsibility.[64]

Much more difficult to interrelate with business attitudes were the extracurricular activities, like athletics, which during this period became an enduring characteristic of college life. Even Veblen, for all his derision of sport and fraternities, came up with ambiguous conclusions. After first blaming the "barbaric" phenomena of sports and the "predatory impulse" of fraternities on the students, he pointed out that both were related to the "sporting and gambling habit" which he had ascribed earlier to the leisure or wealthy class.[65] Such uncertainty arose perhaps from Veblen's effort to be both

[62] Oct. 30, 1881; *Report of the Committee* [on Education and Labor] *of the Senate . . . 1885*, III, 159.

[63] E. J. James, *op. cit.*, p. 33.

[64] Hofstadter and Metzger, *op. cit.*, pp. 374–376.

[65] *Op. cit.*, pp. 378–379.

historian and systematic schemer. The responsible statements of businessmen about athletics, for instance, are
in reality few. Wharton wished to encourage them at
his school within moderate limits "as tending to vigor
and self-reliance." [66] But with all his omniscience in the
design and construction of his university plant, Stanford failed to provide a gymnasium and playing fields.[67]
Though it is implausible to believe that undergraduate
activities were a part of a business design for transform-
ing the higher learning, their adventitious appearance on
campus might make college education more acceptable
to the business community. In certainly one of the most
penetrating reminiscences of undergraduate life ever
written in America, Henry Seidel Canby recalls the
Yale of the nineties:

There never was a more strenuous preparation for active life
anywhere than in the American college of those days. . . .
The cry in our undergraduate world was always "do something," "What does he *do?*" Freshmen hurried up and down
entry stairs seeking news for the college paper, athletes,
often with drawn, worried faces, struggled daily to get or
hold places on the teams, boys with the rudiments of business ability were managers of magazines, orchestras, teams,
or co-operative pants-pressing companies. Those who had
a voice sang, not for sweet music's sake, but to "make"
the glee club. . . . No one that I remember did anything
that was regarded as doing, for its own sake. No, the goal
was prestige, social preferment, a senior society which
would be a spring board to Success in Life. . . . We were

[66] E. J. James, *op. cit.*, p. 32.   [67] Elliott, *op. cit.*, p. 188.

prepared to create a trust or organize a war, not to control the one for human uses and to stop the other before it began.[68]

At the college as at the school level, the emphasis upon character and upon the nature of the moral and mental training received made a good share of the arguments over the subject matter, once the strictly vocational was disregarded, an irrelevance. Along the line of discipline and training alone, the college could appeal to business. Charles F. Thwing, president of Western Reserve and one peculiarly sensitive to impulses from the outside world, announced:

The four qualities most needed in practical concerns one might say are judgment, energy, tact, patience. They are the foundation on which the four-square house of business is built. The college helps to construct each of these walls. It builds the wall of judgment, for it trains one to see, to discriminate, to relate, to infer. It builds the wall of energy, for it creates and conserves strength, enlarges resources, dissipates fear, and enriches power. It builds the wall of tact, for it trains the gentleman. It builds the wall of patience for it lifts the heart away from the impact of to-day onto the appreciation of yesterday and the vision of to-morrow.[69]

[68] *Alma Mater, The Gothic Age of the American College* (New York: Farrar & Rinehart, 1936), pp. 37–43. Quotation reprinted by permission of Rinehart & Company.

[69] "The College as a Preparation for Practical Affairs," *The American College, A Series of Papers Setting Forth the Program, Achievements, Present Status, and Probable Future of the American College* (New York: Holt, 1915), p. 103. Quotation reprinted by permission of the publisher.

What did the customers think? Working in the nineteen-twenties with an adequate sample of business leaders, some of whom were born as early as 1860, F. W. Taussig and C. S. Joslyn concluded, "There has been a trend toward an increasing proportion of college graduates among business leaders in the United States." [70] And focusing on a single institution, his Alma Mater Williams, G. Stanley Hall, a pioneer American psychologist, rejoiced in his autobiography, written in the twenties, that "Williams has long since outgrown those early limitations [of the sixties]. It is today a college for rich quite as much as for poor men." [71] Although the impact of business wish and thought, along with other factors, was making the American college acceptable to the business community, it was far from being inaccepta-ble to the commonalty. Regrettably the new schools cost money. Thus those who approved of M.I.T. on most counts were depressed by the fact that its charges put its education within the reach only of those who were well-to-do and were to become "lieutenants" or "captains" rather than "privates." [72] Stanford, in order to compete with the University of California, consented for a time to let his institution be without tuition charges.[73] In spite of expense, the fact that between

[70] *American Business Leaders: A Study in Social Origins and Social Stratification* (New York: Macmillan, 1932), pp. 163–166.

[71] *Life and Confessions of a Psychologist* (New York: Appleton, 1923), p. 158.

[72] *Report of the Committee* [on Education and Labor] *of the Senate . . . 1885*, III, 159.

[73] Elliott, *op. cit.*, pp. 21, 56, 574.

1872 and 1899–1900 the number of undergraduate collegiate and technical students to each million persons in the United States increased from 573 to 1,233 reveals, *inter alia*, that the trends in higher learning appealed to the people as well as to the tycoon. The study of Taussig and Joslyn came to the same conclusion.[74] The disappearance or modification of a "gentleman's education" shattered a possible social stratification of higher learning.

[74] *Report of the* [U.S.] *Commissioner of Education . . . 1899–1900*, II, 1874; Taussig and Joslyn, *op. cit.*, p. 167.

V

"Sisyphus's Work"

TO FIND the precise word defining the attitude of business toward government is difficult. On the whole it would be too extreme to say that the business community hated or dreaded government; I believe the word "suspected" best covers the various nuances.

One reason for this suspicion was that government action introduced uncertainty into business operations— "I hold the government chiefly responsible for the longer continuance of the present disjointed and irregular commercial state," wrote a representative of business in 1868 [1]—and the removal of uncertainties, be it remem-

[1] E. D. Horton to G. S. Coe, Feb. 28, 1868, Coe Papers, H.B.S.; George Walker to Edward Atkinson, Sept. 29, 1867, Atkinson Papers, M.H.S.

bered, was one of the great business aspirations of the
period. Almost any field of legislation would reveal these
unsettling vacillations—reconstruction policy, currency,
and finance and, above all, the tariff. The well-nigh universal demand on the part of the business community
that the last issue be settled, that something be decided on
a permanent basis, even if it were the wrong decision,
was evidence enough of this charge against government.[2] In the business mind, these government-induced
uncertainties were not a response to inherent pressures
in the situation, nor a legislative adjustment to compli-
cated situations: they were due to the activity of politicians. In order to keep themselves in office, politicians
created fictitious issues, put them up at "auction . . .
for votes," and thus cast misgivings over the future.[3]

The outcome was, of course, an inordinate business
sensitivity to almost any political activity. As *Bradstreet's* put it, toward the end of 1879:

The wheels of industry are revolving at a rapid rate. The
fields have given up their golden harvests; the iron trade
is "booming"; foreign orders are pouring in to such an
extent that a number of idle English steamers have been
chartered by our shippers, and are now on their way across
the water. Activity is permeating every branch of business.
In short, the clouds have passed over, and the sun of pros-

[2] Andrew Carnegie, "Summing up the Tariff Discussion," *North
American Review*, CLI (July, 1890), 74; *Report of the Committee*
[on Education and Labor] *of the Senate . . . 1885*, III, 51–52,
287.

[3] *Twenty-second Annual Report of the Corporation of the
Chamber of Commerce of the State of New York, 1879–'80*, p. 65.

perity is once more shedding its benignant rays upon the United States. Yet there is one little cloud still on the horizon—a mere speck, it is true, but large enough to cause some uneasiness. Congress is to assemble within a few weeks, and the representatives of the people are busily engaged preparing their plans for the session. . . . Let Congress when it assembles, adopt as its motto the now historic words, "Let us have peace." [4]

Since exhortations of this sort usually fell on deaf ears, the Chicago Board of Trade proposed that the presidential term be lengthened to six years in order that the angry discussion and the "upheaval of business in all branches of industry" be spaced at longer intervals than the quadrennial one. Not only was the advent of political activity dreadful, its cessation was a benediction from Providence.[5]

Another corollary of the theory that politics were a disturbance was a dislike for politicians, so frequently referred to in business literature, public and private, as "stupid," "empty," and "noisy," "demagogues," "so-called saviours of the people." [6] Perhaps the unkindest

[4] *Bradstreet's*, XLVII (Oct. 22, 1879), 5.

[5] *Twenty-seventh Annual Report of the Trade and Commerce of Chicago, for the Year Ended December 31, 1884. Compiled for the Board of Trade*, p. xii; *Twenty-first Annual Report of the Corporation of the Chamber of Commerce of the State of New York, 1878–'79*, p. 15.

[6] J. E. Caldwell, *Recollections of a Life Time* (Nashville, Tenn.: Baird-Ward Press, 1923), p. 211; Edward Atkinson, *The Industrial Progress of the Nation: Consumption Limited, Production Unlimited* (New York: Putnam, 1890), pp. 271–272; John Ott to Edward Atkinson, Aug. 21, 1881, Atkinson Papers, M.H.S.

cut of all, considering a businessman made it, was the accusation that politics was "managed by men who devote themselves to it in order to gain a livelihood." [7] From bases such as these it was easy to vault into the daydream that government action should operate in an atmosphere of nonpartisanship.[8]

The second great count against government was its expense. Since there was no way of taking care of these costs aside from placing their burden on the economy, government expenditures were a tax upon the process of production or distribution.[9] On this score the businessmen of that generation were in a position to effect real economies in the amount of government expenditures which they realized arose primarily for military purposes, past or present. Luckily the outcome of the Civil War had been a triumph for union; the Potomac did not become another Rhine, and North and South did not have to maintain large standing armies. If it had been otherwise, Edward Atkinson was calculating in the eighties that, on the basis of American population and

[7] A. S. Hewitt, "Liberty, Learning, and Property," Allan Nevins, ed., *Selected Writings of Abram S. Hewitt* (New York: Columbia University Press, 1937), p. 328.

[8] S. B. Walker to G. S. Coe, Feb. 8, 1868, Coe Papers, H.B.S.; F. W. Bradbury to Edward Atkinson, Aug. 4, 1880, Atkinson Papers, M.H.S.; *Commercial and Financial Chronicle*, LVIII (May 12, 1894), 794–795; H. A. Hill, "The Relations of the Business Men of the United States to the National Legislation," *Journal of Social Science*, III (1871), 155–157.

[9] *Commercial and Financial Chronicle*, XVII (Aug. 30, 1873), 270–271; XVIII (Jan. 3, 1874), 2–3, (May 2, 1874), 442–443; XX (Jan. 16, 1875), 49–50; XXII (Feb. 19, 1876), 171.

the ratio of population to armed forces in France and Germany, the United States would have to maintain a standing army of 700,000.

More than one in twenty of all the adult males of working age within the limits of the country would be withdrawn from their productive work, whereby the quantity of things to be divided between labor and capital, from each year's annual product would be so much diminished. Yet more: one more man in every nineteen of those remaining would be forced to labor in order to pay the taxes necessary to sustain the seven hundred thousand idle men gathered together in camp and barracks waiting for the work of destruction.[10]

The navy of that period was not an expense requiring comparable calculation. As Atkinson wrote to the Secretary of the Treasury, the tax on whisky met the civil expense of the government. "The navy floats on beer—when we have any navy to float—and a surplus over."[11] If among the later men of peace in the business community, Andrew Carnegie for instance, a rational revulsion against the barbarism of throat-cutting and a desire to associate oneself in an "honorific" fashion, as Veblen would say, with very important people, seem the chief motives for joining the peace movement,[12] even Carnegie hinted an antithesis between "industrial

[10] *Report of the Committee* [on Education and Labor] *of the Senate . . . 1885,* II, 223, 236.

[11] Edward Atkinson to C. S. Fairchild, Nov. 6, 1885, Atkinson Papers, M.H.S.

[12] *Autobiography of Andrew Carnegie* (Boston: Houghton, 1920), pp. 282–286, 371.

ideals" and war "ideals." [13] Edward Ginn, businessman, philanthropist, and founder of the World Peace Foundation, was also distressed at costs "in blood and treasure." [14] The reluctance of the business community to embark the nation upon the Spanish-American War, its tardiness in appreciating the advantages of colonial expansion, the outbursts of Theodore Roosevelt, the leader of the jingoes, against Wall Street and "business principles" are too well-known and accepted to require further demonstration. [15]

That the business argument against war penetrated even to the study, Henry Adams, the historian, revealed in a summing up of the American experiment in his famous history of the Jefferson administration:

The success of the American system . . . was a question of economy. If they could relieve themselves from debts, taxes, armies, and government interference with industry, they must succeed in outstripping Europe in economy of production; and Americans were even then partly aware that, if their machine were not so weakened by these economies as to break down in the working, it must of necessity break down every rival. [16]

[13] "Americanism versus Imperialism," *North American Review*, CXLVIII (Jan., 1899), 5.

[14] "Organizing the Peace Work," *World Peace Foundation*, Pamphlet Series III, No. 7, Pt. 1 (July, 1913), p. 3.

[15] Julius Pratt, *Expansionists of 1898. The Acquisition of Hawaii and the Spanish Islands* (Baltimore: Johns Hopkins Press, 1936), pp. 230–278; Carnegie, *Autobiography*, pp. 361–365.

[16] *History of the United States during the First Administration of Thomas Jefferson* (New York: Scribner, 1921), I, 162–163.

Notice that Henry Adams specified one other pre-requisite for any American hegemony besides free-dom from frigates or standing armies, the absence of "government interference with the economy." On this score the business community formulated its most mas-sive indictment against government. The great defect of government was that it continually strayed from its proper sphere; it constantly sought to direct economic affairs by statute law rather than leaving them to natural law. The correct area for government activity was the protection of life and property, the administration of justice, and the "accomplishment of purposes which cannot be worked by individuals." [17] Business spokes-men were usually more specific and more tolerant when they focused on some area other than the national gov-ernment; they then looked with favor upon the making of common highways, the maintenance of common schools, the passage of sanitary regulations, the regula-tion of prices on a local basis for gas, water, and horse-car transportation.[18] These matters of the proper sphere of government action it is as enlightening to define in negative terms as in positive ones. The government, in brief, should not attempt to regulate prices of silver, of labor, of goods, of railroad service; all these are deter-mined in the end by the law of supply and demand; to interfere with its operation by statute law was "arbi-

[17] *Report of the Committee* [on Education and Labor] *of the Senate . . . 1885*, II, 235.

[18] Perkins, Memo, Jan. 26, 1885, Perkins Private Letters and Memos, R.C.O.; Perkins to Cullom Committee, Sept. 21, 1885, *ibid.*

trary," "artificial," and "violent." [19] Furthermore it
was futile. Carnegie regretted: "Our governors, all over
the world, are at Sisyphus's work—ever rolling the
stone uphill to see it roll back to its proper bed at the
bottom." [20] Another favorite figure of speech was: "to
enact that water should of its own accord run up hill," or
"attempting to be wiser than the Creator." [21] From efforts to tinker with or supersede natural law, it followed
that the results sought by statute law were temporary.
Sooner or later the great natural tides which control affairs in the world would reassert themselves.[22] To buck
natural law was to be inefficient. Thus, in case the government regulated railroads, "then imperfect agents of
the government, with no pecuniary interest at stake,
would take the place of imperfect agents of the railroad
companies who are now under the strongest pressure
. . . to make the roads pay a profit, if possible." [23] Mis-
directed government activity defying natural law also
corrupts the people.

[19] Perkins, Memo, May 8, 1885, *ibid.*

[20] *Triumphant Democracy; or Fifty Years' March of the Republic* (New York: Scribner, 1886), p. 48.

[21] *Report of the Committee* [on Education and Labor] *of the
Senate . . . 1885*, II, 153.

[22] Edward Atkinson, *Addresses upon the Labor Question: To
the Workingmen of Providence* (Boston: Franklin Press, 1886);
Perkins, Memo, Dec. 20, 1884(?), Perkins Private Letters and
Memos, R.C.O.; Perkins to Classification Committee of the Western Railroads, Oct., 1885, *ibid.*; Hewitt to Donalson Caffrey, April
17, 1887, Nevins, *op. cit.*, p. 364.

[23] Perkins to Cullom Committee, Sept. 21, 1883, Perkins Private
Letters and Memos, R.C.O.

If a nation legislates a lie and forces its promise of a dollar under a legal-tender act into use in place of the coined metal that carries its own value in its own substance, the people will follow the example; fraud will prevail more and yet more among them until bankruptcy or anarchy forces a return to right methods of legislation.[24]

Through this whole antithesis between natural and statute law runs the American tradition of a higher law. The potentialities of this concept for anarchy and lawlessness have often been demonstrated in American history. It is, however, somewhat of a curiosity that a wide charity in judgment has been shown to those who on the grounds of a higher law outrightly defied the Fugitive Slave Law or condoned John Brown's attack upon a Federal arsenal at Harper's Ferry and none to railroad men who, finding business regulation "unnatural," nibbled away at the long-and-short-haul clause of the Interstate Commerce Act or to manufacturers who on the same stated grounds did not conform to all the provisions of state Factory Acts.

These statements of the proper sphere of government activity are the doctrinaire liberal ones: this does not mean they were not widely accepted and believed. They were. In the circumstances, dissent from them on the part of businessmen is as startling as a thunder clap. For the record, Charles D. McDuffie, agent of cotton mills in Manchester, New Hampshire, informed the Senate Committee on Education and Labor in 1885 that, "you

[24] Edward Atkinson, "The Unlearned Professions," *Atlantic Monthly*, XLV (June, 1880), 745.

certainly can affect business by laws," that legislative interference with natural law "cannot be otherwise" than "useful and beneficial," and that as for himself he did not accept the "natural condition of things as indispensable" but "of course . . . would try to improve it by human agency." [25] Such heresies were rare indeed. Then and since, many other commentators were also sure that the business community's practice demonstrated it had quite other theories of government's sphere than it professed. For instance, it sought and obtained protective tariffs. These set prices; these embodied that active policy of protection and subsidy which later historians have so often declared was the dominant feature of legislation in the years of the robber baron and so contrary to the universal insistence of the latter upon the let-alone policy. Some businessmen of that time apprehended the danger of this ideological incongruity. Edward Atkinson asked:

Has not the tendency ever since the adoption of the protective tariff of 1824 been for many great bodies of the people to think they could better their condition either by attaining higher wages, by shortening the hours of labor, or by some other artificial method, through an appeal to the Legislature to pass every kind of act for regulating the direction of labor, the hours of work, the rate of interest, and the methods of life at every point? Has not the long-continued existence of this system given a tendency to

[25] *Report of the Committee* [on Education and Labor] *of the Senate . . . 1885*, III, 51.

the hardly disguised socialistic movements of the present day? [26]

In actuality, the protective tariff was far from being a policy unanimously accepted by businessmen. Atkinson himself protested against it "as a citizen and a manufacturer," [27] and the individuals, like David A. Wells, who bent their talents to tariff reform or reduction, often expressed their dismay at the passionate extent to which interests other than capitalists, for instance farmers and workers, had become committed to protection.[28]

What then should government do? It should not try to bend or break "fixed and immutable laws" to conform with "pet theories" or "individual prejudices." It should make an effort to "detect and bring to light" the lines along which "natural and fundamental principles are operative and then look for improvement by striving to put ourselves more nearly in harmony with them." [29] If this injunction seemed to reduce the government to

[26] "What Shall Be Taxed? What Shall Be Exempt?" in *The Industrial Progress of the Nation*, pp. 262–263; Perkins to J. S. Martin, Aug., 1877, Perkins Private Letters and Memos, R.C.O.

[27] Atkinson to Merrick, Nov. 18, 1887, Atkinson Papers, M.H.S.; Hewitt to W. L. Wilson, Nov. 15, 1893, Nevins, *op. cit.*, p. 359; *Report of the Committee* [on Education and Labor] *of the Senate . . . 1885*, II, 24.

[28] Letter to Edward Atkinson, Dec. 14, 1880, Atkinson Papers, M.H.S.; J. E. Horr to Edward Atkinson, 1867(?), *ibid.*; *Report of the Committee* [on Education and Labor] *of the Senate . . . 1885*, I, 696–697, 1122–1123; II, 9.

[29] Henry Wood, *Natural Law in the Business World* (Boston: Lee and Shepard, 1887), p. 6.

mere administration, well and good. Addressing the New York Chamber of Commerce at their annual banquet at Delmonico's in 1877, Governor Tilden, responding to the toast to the State of New York, confessed, "I am, myself, a little depressed this evening, and yet a little joyous, for I have just left at Albany 270 bills that are to become laws or be rejected, and on which I have to pass in the next twenty odd days. But when I think of the several hundred bills that were not passed, my melancholy turns into joy." His hearers replied with laughter and applause.[30] Actually the government was not simply to stay its hand; its duty was to remove obstructions upon the operation of natural laws. Automatically this would seem to imply that the community could arrive within foreseeable calculation at the millennium. This was not so. Since even acts designed to remove obstructions could in turn obstruct, the process of unraveling might continue into infinity.[31]

All this thought seems to be mere negativism. In reality there was a positive, even a utopian cast to the business community's attitude toward government. The shrinkage of government's sphere enlarged that within which the self-help and self-reliance of the individual operated. Nor was this all. With many a variation, business spokesmen said that it was the function of

[30] *Nineteenth Annual Report of the Chamber of Commerce of the State of New York*, p. 14.

[31] F. Newman to G. S. Coe, Feb. 1, 1868; T. P. Handy to G. S. Coe, Feb. 6, 1868, Coe Papers, H.B.S.; Edward Atkinson, *Addresses on the Labor Question*, p. 6; *Report of the Committee* [on Education and Labor] *of the Senate . . . 1885*, III, 342.

government to give the individual an equal chance. In the last analysis, they insisted upon the abolition of privilege and the establishment of equality of opportunity.[32] As a reform program, though this lacked the novelty and rhetoric of those proposed by "philanthropists, Professors, and Lady Millionaires," it was as noble in its conception and required more dedication in practice. The iron-master, Abram S. Hewitt, who, as son-in-law of Peter Cooper, was far removed from either the stuffed shirt or the Tory reactionary, lamented the popular hostility to corporations:

It is curious that the mass of the people of this country should fail to recognize their best friends, because corporations have been the only barrier between the despotism of ignorance and the invasion of the rights of property. Doubtless they abuse their privileges at times, but they alone have the ability and the courage to resist attack, and they are doing the work which was done by Jefferson and Madison in the early years of the Republic.[33]

Of all the departments of government, the legislative presented the greatest problem to the business community. Not having had the opportunity of reading the numerous later analyses by historians, economists, and political scientists proving that political power always

[32] *Twenty-eighth Annual Report of the Trade and Commerce of Chicago, for the Year Ended December 31, 1885. Compiled for the Board of Trade,* p. xii; Hewitt, "Liberty, Learning and Property," Nevins, *op. cit.,* pp. 318–319.

[33] Letter to R. D. Haislip, June 16, 1898, Nevins, *op. cit.,* p. 369; Hewitt, "Liberty, Learning, and Property," *ibid.,* pp. 317–318.

gravitates into the hands of dominant economic groups, the businessmen of the era did not have that comfort; they relied instead upon their personal experience. Capitalists and employers concluded that they were a minority, and since they were too preoccupied to give much time to legislation and were rarely directly represented in the legislature, they believed that the lobby maintained by other interests was larger and more persistent.[34] Of course eminent businessmen had an advantage in the fact that very important people flock together; politicians in the upper brackets naturally associated with their opposite numbers in business. Businessmen wrote to and talked to influential politicians, counseled them, and often did them favors. But the outcome under our system of government could not be counted on. With a note of jubilation, Edward Atkinson wrote after a visit from a key Senator, "Mr. Allison of Iowa has been here for a few days. . . . He was all wrong about paper money and is now all right. I think I can claim him as my convert and I, therefore, feel well paid for my work as he will have great influence in the next Com. of Ways & Means." [35] But only three months earlier Allison had summarized his philosophy for Mr. Atkinson: "I always like to vote, if I can, so as not to be called upon to explain too much at home." [36]

[34] *Report of the Committee* [on Education and Labor] *of the Senate . . . 1885*, II, 332.

[35] Edward Atkinson to J. M. Forbes, Aug. 16, 1867, Atkinson Papers, M.H.S.

[36] W. B. Allison to Edward Atkinson, March 8, 1867, *ibid.*

In the end the problem of the legislature was the problem of the "people back home"; it was the problem of the majority and its relation to its representatives. When speaking of majorities, businessmen were apt to employ the words "brutal," "selfish," and "ignorant." [37] Even Carnegie, who phrased the dedication of his shallow volume, *Triumphant Democracy*, "To the Beloved Republic under whose equal laws I am made the peer of any man, although denied political equality by my native land, I dedicate this book with an intensity of gratitude and admiration which the native-born citizen can neither feel nor understand," [38] asserted elsewhere in its pages that the voice of the people was not always the voice of God.[39] As for the relationships between the people and their chosen representatives, business opinion fell into two schools. One asserted that statesmen "pandered to the caprices" of their constituents; [40] the other that statesmen did not represent the true wishes of the electorate. At first glance these contradictory interpretations would seem to imply that business thought on the matter was merely opportunistic. Though this inference was often true, it was possible to harmonize the attitudes. In the end, or on sober second thought, the people were right: their spokesmen represented mean-

[37] Sidney Homer to G. S. Coe, Jan. 21, 1868, Coe Papers, H.B.S.; *Report of the Committee* [on Education and Labor] *of the Senate . . . 1885*, I, 1089–1090.

[38] Carnegie, *Triumphant Democracy*, dedication page.

[39] *Ibid.*, p. 365.

[40] J. E. Horr to Edward Atkinson, 1867(?), Atkinson Papers, M.H.S.

while the transient wishes of the people.[41] What could bring the people to their senses? First of all, obviously, the passage of time.[42] Others less sanguine felt disaster or crisis was necessary. "While I have faith in the people," wrote John S. Gray to George S. Coe,

I cannot help remembering that they do not move until the mischief is done & they feel the consequences in their pockets & in their daily bread. . . . When we are flat on our backs, financially and commercially, then the ability will be drawn out and developed & the people at large, men of property, will turn away from politicians, asking "Who shall show us any good," and will listen to the dictates of experience & of sound financial principles.[43]

But the most common hope lay elsewhere. As a New England land agent in the West said, "In this good, democratic country where every man is allowed to vote, the intelligence and the property of the country is at the mercy of the ignorant, idle and vicious. A republican government is worse than a monarchy when not based on the intelligence and virtue of the people." [44] Education brought people to their senses and showed

[41] Edward Atkinson, "Remedies for Social Ills," *Forum,* VII (April, 1889), 161–162; Carnegie, *Triumphant Democracy,* p. 365.

[42] Perkins, Memo, June 6, 1905, Perkins Private Letters and Memos, R.C.O.

[43] Feb. 14, 1868, Coe Papers, H.B.S.

[44] Quoted in Larry Gara, "Cyrus Woodman, A Westernized Yankee," p. 290, MS thesis (University of Wisconsin); S. G. Lanier to G. S. Coe, Feb. 10, 1868, Coe Papers, H.B.S.; Hewitt, "Liberty, Learning, and Property," Nevins, *op. cit.,* p. 329.

them their true self-interest. We have already noted how this realization operated in the history of the public schools. It was the "true panacea for all the ills of the body politic."[45] But no school system operated to inform or convert adult voters. In a democracy business, if it were to have its way, must continuously educate those who had ballots.

On the score of their private business affairs, some of the titans were slow to recognize this necessity. Originally Rockefeller innocently believed the accomplishments of the Standard Oil Company would answer the critics and, when Miss Tarbell delivered her powerful attacks in the muckraking history of Standard Oil, stood firm with the reply, "Not a word! Not a word about that misguided woman."[46] Lower down in the business hierarchy, the president of the Norfolk and Western Railroad thought it no disgrace to be disliked: "It sounds odd to talk of a railroad president as being popular, as if he was a comedian or a politician."[47] On matters of public policy, however, the business community in general realized the necessity of educating the people, and it undertook the task on a wide scale. Businessmen made speeches, and they wrote articles, for

[45] Carnegie, *Triumphant Democracy*, p. 101.

[46] J. T. Flynn, *God's Gold: The Story of Rockefeller and His Times* (New York: Harcourt, Brace, 1932), pp. 389–390; R. W. and M. E. Hidy, *Pioneering in Big Business, 1882–1911* (New York: Harper, 1955), pp. 642–654.

[47] J. T. Lambie, *From Mine to Market: The History of Coal Transportation on the Norfolk and Western Railway* (New York: New York University Press, 1954), p. 22.

which the editors of the respectable periodicals of the era, the *Forum*, the *North American Review*, the *Atlantic*, the *Century*, clamored. These verbal and written statements in turn attracted newspapermen and were either reprinted or summarized in their journals or called for notice and editorializing.[48] Sometimes an economic interest would reprint and distribute this material in pamphlet or book. Thus, even without the purchase of a newspaper, as Tom Scott and Jay Gould had purchased the New York *World*, or without subsidization, as Standard Oil had subsidized *Gunton's Magazine*,[49] businessmen knew how to secure a hearing.

Associated, they had even more influence. The Chamber of Commerce of the State of New York described itself as a "corporate body, influencing public opinion." [50] Sometimes businessmen and their allies brought into being *ad hoc* associations. Thus in 1880, a group of businessmen, publishers, and educators of high prestige founded the Society for Political Education because "the growing tendency of government to enlarge its sphere, and the demands constantly made to increase the power and the responsibility of the STATE, make political education more than ever a supreme necessity for the just limitation and right guidance of governmental authority." Members did not have to subscribe to

[48] Perkins to Edward Atkinson, June 15, 1881, Atkinson Papers, M.H.S.; B. J. Hendrick, *The Life of Andrew Carnegie* (New York: Doubleday, 1932), II, 277–278; D. R. James to G. S. Coe, April 1, 1886, Coe Papers, H.B.S.

[49] Flynn, *op. cit.*, pp. 200–201; Hidy and Hidy, *op. cit.*, pp. 659–661.

[50] *Nineteenth Annual Report . . . 1876-'77*, p. xii.

every item in a detailed creed—which included: (1)
The office must seek the man and not the man the office,
(2) The greenbacks should be redeemed in specie, (3)
Trade has the right to the freest scope, unfettered by
taxes, except for government expenses, (4) Neither the
public money nor the people's land must be used to
subsidize private enterprise—but they did have to fork
in a $1.00 membership fee, which was used to circulate
books at low prices and provide reading lists, both illus-
trating in sound fashion the above cited principles.[51]
While all this did not amount to the "control of the
press" about which the discontented were always com-
plaining,[52] it reveals how sharp a break with the past the
muckraking periodicals of the next century really made
and how the business dislike for the yellow journalism
of Pulitzer and Hearst was not based merely on grounds
of refinement and good taste.[53]

Generally the business spokesmen did not direct their
exhortation and explanation to demos, to the "common
man," but to the thoughtful portion of the community.
The latter would filter the opinion down to the rank
and file. Even then, one could not be sure of success.
As one of Coe's correspondents wrote,

Your address ought to go into every farm cottage in the
land, for that is the place of danger. As a rule the laboring

[51] Society for Political Education, *Economic Tracts*, No. XXVIII
(New York: Society for Political Education, 1889), inside cover.
[52] *Report of the Committee* [on Education and Labor] *of the
Senate . . . 1885*, I, 1114–1117; II, 835, 839–840.
[53] Hewitt to V. H. Rothschild, Oct. 23, 1871, Nevins, *op. cit.*,
p. 387.

part of our population, having no time to read, take their opinions from the *four corners*, where the post-office and tavern and blacksmith and store are—or from the village politician who has an axe to grind, and uses any stone he finds useful for the moment.[54]

This analysis of the difficulty of educating or elevating the masses came in the seventies. Nearly thirty years later Charles Elliott Perkins recognized the failure of the businessman's effort to influence the public. "How much good has been done by the talkers? [J. J.] Hill has been talking and telling the truth for the last two or three years, but it has not produced any good effect." "My own letter" to Senator Cullom on the Interstate Commerce Act though prepared by an able group, "did not have as much effect as a fly on a cart wheel."[55]

In view of the deficiencies of legislatures, businessmen tended to look elsewhere in government for an appreciation of correct principles. They found governors and presidents were open to argument and less governed by narrow interests. That such discovery was not in error, President Grant's veto in April, 1874, of a bill authorizing greenbacks and President Hayes's threatened and actual vetoes of silver legislation demonstrated.[56] Perhaps better than governors and presidents were the judges. The businessman's preference for the last was

[54] G. S. Trowbridge, Oct. 7, 1879, Coe Papers, H.B.S.

[55] Perkins to H. L. Higginson, March 20, 1907; Perkins to T. M. Marquett, Jan. 3, 1891, Perkins Private Letters and Memos, R.C.O.

[56] Edward Atkinson, "Veto of the Inflation Bill of 1874," *Journal of Political Economy*, I (Dec., 1892), 117–119.

part ideological, part expedient. Under the first rubric, it was assumed judges had a hieratic function; the jurist, member of "the highest of all professions," is the one who "of right provides against wrong, . . . and by whom the rigid provisions of statute law, imperfect as it must always be, may be alleviated in the Court of Equity." [57] Perhaps Edward Atkinson spoke thus because he had just been awarded an LL.D. by the University of South Carolina. James Caldwell, unsoftened by such graceful recognition, hardly agreed.

I have sat in a court room and witnessed the opera bouffe of a judge listening to evidence, trying to determine the price at which certain services should be sold, all parties utterly oblivious to and unmindful of the fundamental laws which sooner or later make all prices, to wit, supply and demand, use and value.[58]

Still, judges were more remote from the people, better educated and better trained than most government officials. "There are so many jack-asses about now days who think property has no rights, that the filling of Supreme Court vacancies is the most important function of the Presidential office," [59] wrote Charles Elliott Perkins.

[57] "Commencement Address Given to the Graduating Class of the University of South Carolina, June 26, 1889," *The Industrial Progress of the Nation*, pp. 1–2.

[58] *Op. cit.*, p. 185.

[59] Letter to J. M. Forbes, Feb. 21, 1894, Pamphlet, Perkins Collection, R.C.O.; J. W. Hurst, *The Growth of American Law: The Law Makers* (Boston: Little, 1950), pp. 85–146, 170–195; Bliss Perry, *Life and Letters of Henry Lee Higginson* (Boston: Atlantic Monthly Press, 1921), p. 442.

Whether dealing with legislature, executive, court, or bureaucrat, those who believe that money has the loudest voice are easily persuaded that the business community secured its way by graft. According to this canon, the period of the robber barons crawls with lobbyists and pay-off agents plentifully provided with the long green; everyone had a price and quite likely received it. It is possible to question this picture *ab initio*. Like other people, reformers and the foes of business were convinced of their own righteousness and naturally explained the failure of their programs, not in terms of the latter's deficiencies or inacceptability, but in terms of corruption. Nor were boasts by businessmen of their power over legislators and others satisfactory evidence of the prevalence of graft.[60] To these assertions the colloquy in Henry IV is applicable:

GLENDOWER: I can call spirits from the vasty deep.
HOTSPUR: Why so can I, or so can any man;
But will they come when you do call for them?

In short, an assertion of possibilities does not authenticate corruption; proof of it must accord with the traditions of Anglo-Saxon jurisprudence. Another reason for exaggerating the extent of corruption in the period of the robber barons was the persistence of a naïve stereotype of the government process as constituting something apart from life and ideal; hence any endeavor

[60] E. L. Godkin, "Some Political and Social Aspects of the Tariff," *New Princeton Review*, III (March, 1887), 169; Wayne Andrews, *The Vanderbilt Legend: The Story of the Vanderbilt Family* (New York: Harcourt, Brace, 1941), pp. 192, 195.

to inform or persuade a legislator was *ipso facto* sinister and dishonest.[61]

But, as in all ages, there was governmental corruption, a part of which did not involve business enterprise at all. Some blamed the phenomenon on the instinct of legislators to invade the realm of natural law or on the desire of "solons" to blackmail capitalists into buying them off.[62] Abram Hewitt blamed it on the people. Tilden and his friends couldn't reform Tammany Hall. "The people who support Tammany Hall did not want to be reformed. They did not want the government of the people, but they wanted the government of a boss." [63] Furthermore there was in the business community an actual revulsion against the use of money in politics. John Murray Forbes, New England railroad builder and investor, certainly in a position to know what he was talking about, wrote in 1880: "There are many very wealthy men of whom Mr. Salisbury of Worcester is the type who won't give money for politics from a vague & very sound but very *wrong* idea that votes may be bought." [64]

[61] Hurst, *op. cit.*, pp. 62–64; *Report of the Committee* [on Education and Labor] *of the Senate* . . . *1885*, I, 347–351.

[62] Caldwell, *op. cit.*, pp. 182, 184; Perkins, Memo, Jan. 26, 1885; Memo, Oct., 1888, Perkins Private Letters and Memos, R.C.O.; Jonathan Chace to Edward Atkinson, Feb. 25, 1881, Atkinson Papers, M.H.S.

[63] Hewitt to V. H. Rothschild, Oct. 23, 1871, Nevins, *op. cit.*, p. 387.

[64] Letter to Edward Atkinson, July 26, 1880, Atkinson Papers, M.H.S.

In fact the business community was more prone to resort to other devices to check the ignorance and imprudence of the masses or their representatives. One was that new governmental device of the period—the commission. These had the expertness and nonpartisanship the business community craved.[65] The Chicago Board of Trade, caught between agrarian agitators and the practices of railroads running to the seaboard, called for a commission of "high-minded and competent men, wielding the strong arm of national authority, to prevent a reckless competition for traffic, and to adjust the interests of commerce with those of railways." Such a commission would terminate "intemperate and ill-considered discussion." [66] In Massachusetts, the president of an important railroad informed the Railroad Commission:

I had supposed that your honorable corporation was created to, in some measure, stand between the railroad corporations and their patrons. . . . I have not supposed, do not now suppose, that the commission intends to go outside of this high position, or to seriously attempt advising the trained and experienced managers of roads in this Commonwealth upon the details of their duty.[67]

[65] Edward Atkinson, "How Society Reforms Itself," *Forum,* VII (March, 1889), 25–26; C. F. Adams, Jr., "Boston," *North American Review,* CVI (Jan., 1868), 18–19, 25.

[66] *Twenty-seventh Annual Report of the Trade and Commerce of Chicago, for the Year Ended December 31, 1884. Compiled for the Board of Trade,* p. xxvii.

[67] *Third Annual Report of the* [Massachusetts] *Board of Railroad Commissioners, January, 1872,* p. xxxiv.

Although words and tone were arrogant, the statement of the commission's purpose was essentially correct, and the wide popularity of an Advisory Commission of the Massachusetts type shows its general acceptability to the business community.[68]

The second recourse of the business community was a reformed civil service. The contrary notion that businessmen debauched the civil service defies the whole canon of business reasoning in the era. Businessmen disliked expensive government; an ill-organized civil service wasted money. Businessmen wished promptness and dependability of service; the bureaucratic delays and in some cases the outright blackmail of incompetent civil servants was intolerable.[69] The list of early members in the National Civil Service Reform Association contains many businessmen along with professional men and reformers,[70] and George Washington Curtis, president of the Association, was informing the annual meetings, held at Newport, significant spot, that the Association was simply striving for the application to

[68] B. H. Meyer, *Railroad Legislation in the United States* (New York: Macmillan, 1903), pp. 167–186.

[69] D. B. Eaton, *The Spoils System and Civil Service Reform in the Customs House and Post-Office at New York* (New York: Putnam, 1881), p. 45; R. G. Cleland, *A History of Phelps Dodge, 1834–1950* (New York: Knopf, 1952), pp. 59–67; C. F. Adams, Jr., "Boston," *North American Review*, CVI (April, 1868), 583–585; C. R. Fish, *The Civil Service and the Patronage* (Cambridge: Harvard University Press, 1904), pp. 244–245.

[70] Printed Minutes of the Central Committee or Council 1881–1920, National Civil Service League [n.p., n.d.], National Civil Service League Library, New York City.

government business of the sound practices of the "private employer." [71]

Commission and civil service were ways by which an elite, educated in economics and economic history, could get its hands on the governmental process. It is somewhat touching, also, to discover that the pioneers in business education cherished the innocent assumption that their schools could educate both for business and public service. Wharton hoped that as a result of training in his school the sons of wealthy parents could learn to use "property . . . for the benefit of the community or could be drawn into careers of unselfish legislation and administration." Consequently there was much curricular emphasis upon American history and citizenship and upon public as well as private accounts.[72] At Chicago, the proposed School was one not only of Commerce but of Administration, and one aim was the training of diplomats and consuls.[73] And before the

[71] *Proceedings of the Annual Meeting of the National Civil Service Reform League, Held at Newport, Rhode Island, August 1, 1883* (New York: National Civil Service Reform League, 1883), pp. 9, 23.

[72] E. J. James, *An Address before the Convention of the American Bankers' Association at Saratoga, September 3, 1890* (New York: American Bankers' Association, 1892), pp. 13, 17–18, 29–30; Joseph Wharton, *Is a College Education Advantageous to a Business Man? Address Delivered by Joseph Wharton at the Reception Given February 20th, 1890, by the Wharton School Association* [n.p., n.d.], p. 20.

[73] W. R. Harper, *The President's Report: Administration, Decennial Publications* (Chicago: University of Chicago Press, 1903), I, lxxxix–xci.

university finally made up its mind what it should do on the premises, Harvard dallied with the idea of a Graduate School of Public Service and Commerce.[74]

In spite of occasional moments of misgiving over the operation of republican government and reservations on matters of detail, the American business community was feverishly patriotic. Like other men, they could make the eagle scream in praise of American principles and see God in American history. The New York State Chamber of Commerce lapped up nationalistic oratory at its annual banquets, and the relatively matter-of-fact George S. Coe, after surveying the course of American history, declared,

It seems to me immeasurably impious, not to recognize in all this, as in all human history, the guiding hand of a good Providence. But especially here, where we can so clearly perceive the march of events, effecting great results from apparently contrary causes. Our fathers builded better than they knew.[75]

This was in 1885. The events of the next year, the strikes and the Haymarket Bomb Outrage, raised genuine doubts. Lyman J. Gage, president of the First National Bank in Chicago and a person of exceptional poise and perception, wondered if MacCauley's prophecy of an hour of trouble for America might not be coming

[74] W. B. Donham, "The Graduate School of Business Administration," S. E. Morison, ed., *The Development of Harvard University Since the Inauguration of President Eliot, 1869–1929* (Cambridge: Harvard University Press, 1930), pp. 533–534.

[75] MS speech of G. S. Coe on Oct. 20, 1885, Coe Papers, H.B.S.

true. The filling up of the public land and the conges-
tion of population in cities would put "the severest
strain" upon "our democratic institutions." [76] Charles
Elliott Perkins, even before Haymarket, did not see how
it would all end. "When we have two or three times as
many voters as now and few owners of property in
proportion to the whole, there may be troubles which
will upset the whole scheme and make it necessary to
establish one or more strong governments with large
standing armies." [77] Perhaps these statements were but
another example of the social masochism so common in
American life. Populists as well as capitalists found
some release in dreaming of a day of doom and in the
subsequent emergence of a golden age which would re-
solve all difficulties.[78]

Being "practical," businessmen did not give much
time to these apocalyptic day dreams. Gage felt it was
within the potentialities of the economic order, with
its power over nature, to be useful in allaying discontent, not by argument but by demonstration. For Atkinson, the capering of politicians was of little moment.

Our success in resuming our place among nations and in
taking the lead in paying our debts has been due to our merchants, our men of affairs, to our railroad managers, and

[76] "Presidential Address," *Proceedings of the American Bankers'
Association, 1886,* p. 10.

[77] Letters to E. F. Perkins, April 7, 1886, and to W. B. Allison,
April 26, 1880, Perkins Family Papers, VI, R.C.O.

[78] Richard Hofstadter, *The Age of Reform from Bryan to
F.D.R.* (New York: Knopf, 1955), pp. 67–70, 72 n.

our capitalists,—far more than our statesmen. . . . It is the work of those who have produced and distributed our great crops of cotton and of corn that has achieved results.[79]

Those who built the economic order built the nation. Had not the tycoon of them all, John D. Rockefeller, said, "I saw a marvelous future for our country, and I wanted to participate in the work of making our country great. I had an ambition to build." [80] In the broadest conceivable sense, the welfare of the economy assured the safety of the Republic.

[79] Edward Atkinson, "The Unlearned Professions," p. 750; Gage, *op. cit.*, p. 10.

[80] Quoted in Flynn, *op. cit.*, p. 201.

VI

"Don't Shoot the Millionaire"

EARLY in 1889, Allen Thorndike Rice, editor of the *North American Review*, burst into Carnegie's library. He held in his hand a copy of an article entitled "Wealth" which Carnegie had written and sent him. Rice announced it was the finest article he had ever published in the review, asked Carnegie to read it aloud word for word, and perhaps dearest compliment of all, for Carnegie liked to patronize peers, said it would displace the lead article written by Lord Wolseley for the June issue of the magazine.[1] While there is no ac-

[1] "The Best Fields for Philanthropy," *North American Review*, CXLIX (Dec., 1889), 682–683.

counting for editorial effervescence, Rice was justified. The article was not without the touch of that exhibitionism usually displayed in Carnegie's written work—to talk about giving money away, a "personal subject," was, as Rockefeller suspected, "beyond the pale of good taste" [2]—but here the thesis was striking, "The man who dies thus rich dies disgraced," and Carnegie named names to demonstrate it. Actually on this occasion Carnegie wrote with unaccustomed depth and seriousness, for he was trying to convert his fellow millionaires to the Gospel of Wealth.

"There are but three modes in which surplus wealth can be disposed of. It can be left to the family of the decedents; it can be bequeathed for public purposes; or, finally, it can be administered during their lives by its possessors." The first method, an expression of family "vanity," injures the recipients; the second is open to the danger of bequests being perverted and "no man is to be extolled for doing what he cannot help doing." The third way was Carnegie's preachment. It was

the duty of the man of wealth . . . to consider all surplus revenues which come to him simply as trust funds, which he is called upon to administer . . . to produce the most beneficial results for the community—the man of wealth thus becoming the mere agent and trustee for his poorer brethren, bringing to their service his superior wisdom,

[2] J. D. Rockefeller, *Random Reminiscences of Men and Events* (New York: Doubleday, 1933), p. 156.

experience, and ability to administer, doing for them better than they would or could do for themselves.[3]

It might be said, perhaps in derogation, that this preachment so far from being timeless, emerged from the economic context of the day. This was a period of widespread discontent; apprehensive observers saw Socialism and Communism marching forward to confiscate wealth and divide it among "the rabble," this division was a singular obsession of these decades. Carnegie was not loath to admit his lesson was timely. "The problem of our age is the proper administration of wealth, so that the ties of brotherhood may still bind together the rich and poor in harmonious relationship." "Much of this sum [the donation of Cooper to Cooper Union], if distributed in small quantities among the people, would have been wasted in the indulgence of appetite, some of it in excess, and it may be doubted whether even the part put to the best use, that of adding to the comforts of the home, would have yielded results for the race, as a race, at all comparable to those which are flowing and are to flow from the Cooper Institute from generation to generation." [4] Those prone to interpret ideas in terms of the economic conditions of their formulators might be able to say the Gospel of Wealth was the response of a man whose fortune had grown so great that he could no longer get rid of it

[3] "Wealth," *North American Review*, CXLVIII (June, 1889), 657–662.

[4] *Ibid.*, pp. 653, 660–661.

by a "retail business" of giving—sums in the order of magnitude of $5,000—at which Carnegie sneered.[5] But Carnegie's much earlier decisions on the critical need of giving away his surplus, and the fact that his surplus was now nowhere near as great as later, and that this article was an article and not a donation, would seem to modify this interpretation. Carnegie was now announcing a general and enduring doctrine, also an epochal one. He transformed "giving," consecrated over centuries as charity, into philanthropy.

The differences between charity and philanthropy were not merely matters of scale; they were matters of kind. Taking a cue from a later distinguished maker of distinctions, F. D. Roosevelt, we can call charity relief and philanthropy reform. This meant that the new program looked to the improvement of the future rather than the amelioration of the past. Or as John D. Rockefeller put it, "The best philanthropy is constantly in search of the finalities—a search for cause, an attempt to cure evils at their source." [6] In a later article Carnegie catalogued the proper objectives of philanthropy: universities—though "the use for many, or perhaps any, new universities does not exist" —astronomical observatories, library buildings, institutions like hospitals and laboratories for the alleviation of human suffering, concert halls, public baths, parks, and ornamental buildings including conservatories "filled with beautiful flowers,

[5] B. J. Hendrick, *The Life of Andrew Carnegie* (New York: Doubleday, 1932), II, 260.
[6] *Op. cit.,* p. 177.

orchids, and aquatic plants which they [the working-men], with their wives and children can enjoy in their spare hours." [7] Certainly this last suggestion of conservatories epitomizes the distance between charity and philanthropy.

Furthermore charity was outside the realm of natural law; it was personal in origin,[8] while philanthropy operated within the area of natural law. It was natural law which enabled the huge fortunes to be accumulated in the first place; the disposal of these sums aided recipients to help themselves, another commendable aspect of natural law. This latter process was sometimes assisted by the habit of conditional gifts from the givers. Although the idea of self-help under philanthropy might simply perpetuate the idea that the giver under charity must not pauperize individuals,[9] the former way of giving was also an illustration of the natural law that wealth tends to reproduce itself. It cannot be emphasized too strongly that philanthropy grew out of the laws of the economic order—"Individualism, Private Property, the Law of Accumulation of Wealth, and the Law of Competition" [10]—and was one of the justifica-

[7] "The Best Fields for Philanthropy," pp. 687–696; *Report of the Committee* [on Education and Labor] *of the Senate . . . 1885,* I, 73.

[8] C. E. Perkins, Memo, 1882; Memo, Jan. 17, 1885; Memo, Jan. 26, 1885, Perkins Private Letters and Memos, R.C.O.; *Nation,* XLIII (Dec. 30, 1886), p 538.

[9] A. S. Hewitt to editor of the New York *Sun,* Jan. 9, 1901, Allan Nevins, ed., *Selected Writings of Abram S. Hewitt* (New York: Columbia University Press, 1937), p. 375.

[10] Carnegie, "Wealth," p. 657.

tions for the way they operated. Finally charity was usually associated with Christian stewardship; philanthropy was secular. Carnegie announced: "The highest life is probably to be reached, not by such imitation of the life of Christ as Count Tolstoï gives us, but, while animated by Christ's spirit, . . . still laboring for the good of our fellows, which was the essence of his life and teaching, but laboring in a different manner." [11] Nor did Carnegie approve of giving money to churches; they were not the community. Perhaps an exception might be made to improve the level of ecclesiastical architecture! [12] The angry buzz of churchmen and hurt correction by them in response to Carnegie's original article—his most embattled critic characterized him as an "anti-Christian phenomenon" [13]—was further proof of philanthropy's secular tone.

There is a temptation to add that Carnegie's Gospel of Wealth was peculiarly American. Among the commentators on his creed was William Ewart Gladstone. In a dreary article, which nevertheless elevated Carnegie's self-esteem, the British Prime Minister inferred a dis-

---

[11] *Ibid.*, p. 661.

[12] Carnegie, "The Best Fields for Philanthropy," p. 696.

[13] Cardinal Gibbons, "Wealth and Its Obligations," *North American Review*, CLII (April, 1891), 387–393; H. C. Potter, "The Gospel for Wealth," *North American Review*, CLII (May, 1891), 522; Henry Edward Cardinal Manning, H. P. Hughes, Hermann Adler, "Irresponsible Wealth," *Nineteenth Century*, XXVIII (Dec., 1890), 884–885, 886–887, 891–892. A much more probing criticism was W. J. Tucker, "The Gospel of Wealth," *Andover Review*, XV (June, 1891), 631–645.

tinction between America and England by summarizing
the advantages of connecting wealth with family and ex-
tolling the operation of *noblesse oblige*, "recognized responsibility to others," in a country "of old wealth" and
wealthy landowners.[14] Unfortunately for the theory of
Americanism, Carnegie's ablest critic in the United
States thought American wealth was already displaying a sense of *noblesse oblige* and thus muted Gladstone's
distinctions.[15]

His clerical commentators were sure that Carnegie's
declaration was novel, "absolutely unique," as Bishop
Potter put it.[16] Carnegie himself did not thus lose per-
spective. Wealthy men in America before him had
given great sums displaying the stigmata of true philanthropy. Although Girard's "well-meaning" donation of
six millions had gone to a college and to the city of
Philadelphia and had flaunted the Philadelphian's anti-
clericalism, and although Tilden's five millions had gone
for a public library in New York City, unhappily both
had fallen short of perfection by being bequests. They
were not administered by the givers in their lifetime.[17]
Yet Carnegie found "true disciples of the Gospel of

[14] "Mr. Carnegie's Gospel of Wealth," *Nineteenth Century*,
XXVIII (Nov., 1890), 683–685.

[15] E. J. Phelps, "Irresponsible Wealth," *North American Review*,
CLII (May, 1891), 532–533. But see E. L. Godkin, "The Expenditure of Rich Men," *Scribner's Magazine*, XX (Oct., 1896), 500.

[16] *Op. cit.*, p. 514.

[17] Carnegie, "Wealth," p. 661; Andrew Carnegie, *Ezra Cornell:
An Address to the Students of Cornell University on Ezra Cornell
Day, April Twenty-sixth, 1907*, pp. 14–18.

Wealth" in Senator Stanford, Enoch Pratt of Baltimore and Charles Pratt of Brooklyn, and above all Peter Cooper.[18] Though the latter's son-in-law, Abram Hewitt, professed to believe Carnegie's ideas were innovations, Cooper seems, though he kept God in the picture, to have anticipated in speech and practice most of Carnegie's precepts of philanthropy.[19] Later Carnegie added Ezra Cornell to his Valhalla of philanthropists, because he gave a public library to Ithaca—"I shall not be expected to disagree with our hero upon that point"— established Cornell with its emphasis upon science and engineering, and "although not quite orthodox in his day, was mindful of the great truth that the highest worship of God is service to man!"[20] Wide as he swung his dragnet for disciples, it is far from clear that Carnegie's enumeration included every predecessor.[21] He may also have derived his philosophy of wealth from popular attitudes. When John Jacob Astor died in 1848, there was intense curiosity about his will, and apparently so convinced were editors and reformers that he should give money for public purposes that they felt entitled to regard his $400,000 bequest for a free public library as inadequate and stingy.[22]

[18] "Wealth," pp. 660–661, 663; Carnegie, "The Best Fields for Philanthropy," pp. 685, 687–696.

[19] E. C. Mack, *Peter Cooper: Citizen of New York* (New York: Duell, Sloan and Pearce, 1949), pp. 250–251.

[20] *Ezra Cornell*, pp. 14, 18, 25.

[21] Abraham Flexner, *Funds and Foundations* (New York: Harper, 1952), pp. 9–23.

[22] Sigmund Diamond, *The Reputation of the American Business Man* (Cambridge: Harvard University Press, 1955), pp. 31 ff.

When Carnegie issued his thesis without an accompanying concrete munificence, Rockefeller was maturing his first large gift to the University of Chicago. It was known in May, 1889, just a month before Carnegie published his "Wealth." [23] As the oil king continued to pour forth millions for one philanthropy or another, he paused long enough to write Carnegie that he approved the latter's expression of "sentiments" and to acknowledge the importance of his example.[24] Indeed, Rockefeller's statement of his creed for giving parallels in a striking way the Carnegie concept of philanthropy. Although his own generosities had matured within a Baptist chrysalis and he was constantly being advised by Baptist clergymen, Rockefeller shied away from purely Christian giving—"The man who plans to do all his giving on Sunday is a poor prop for the institutions of the country" [25]—and preferred to charity the scientific attack on underlying conditions. Rockefeller was more favorably impressed than Carnegie with education as a proper object of philanthropy. On one point of high theory he was indeed somewhat more explicit than Carnegie:

Up to the present time no scheme has yet presented itself which seems to afford a better method of handling capital than that of individual ownership. We might put our money into the Treasury of the Nation and of the various states,

[23] Allan Nevins, *Study in Power: John D. Rockefeller, Industrialist and Philanthropist* (New York: Scribner, 1953), II, 156–158, 220, 300–302.
[24] Rockefeller, *op. cit.*, p. 166; Hendrick, *op. cit.*, I, 349.
[25] *Op. cit.*, p. 142.

but we do not find any promise in the National or state legislatures, viewed from the experiences of the past, that the funds would be expended for the general weal more effectively than under the present methods, nor do we find in any of the schemes of socialism a promise that wealth would be more wisely administered for the general good.[26]

Though Carnegie and Rockefeller worked hard and systematically on their benefactions, their real life was the production of goods and services. And it was by this test they wanted finally to be judged. As Rockefeller put it,

The best philanthropy, the help that does the most good and the least harm, the help that nourishes civilization at its very root, that most widely disseminates health, righteousness, and happiness, is not what is usually called charity. It is, in my judgment, the investment of effort or time or money, carefully considered with relation to the power of employing people at a remunerative wage, to expand and develop the resources at hand, and to give opportunity for progress and healthful labour where it did not exist before. No mere money-giving is comparable to this in its lasting and beneficial results.[27]

To this idea that the capitalist performed his greatest service by putting people to work, Rockefeller and others returned again and again.[28] The best philanthropy

[26] *Ibid.*, pp. 145–160, 177.
[27] J. D. Rockefeller, *Random Reminiscences of Men and Events* (copyright, 1909 by Doubleday, Page & Company; copyright, 1937 by John D. Rockefeller), pp. 141, 142. Reprinted by permission.
[28] *Ibid.*, pp. 143–145; Phelps, *op. cit.*, pp. 528–529.

was the pay roll. This arrangement helped people to help themselves; this was the true alternative to confiscatory taxes, government expenditures, and socialism.[29]

In parading their other economic accomplishments, businessmen looked upon people not as employees but as consumers. For the latter industrial and business advance had provided a constantly increasing quantity of goods at lower prices; the luxuries of yesterday had been made the necessities of the present. With a unanimity that was impressive, apologists picked upon one of the superficially most unpromising specimens among capitalists to demonstrate this benign process, Commodore Vanderbilt, proud ruler of the New York Central. In 1865 the cost of moving a barrel of flour one thousand miles from the interior of the country to the seaboard was $3.45; in 1885 it was 68 cents. Throughout the country each adult person used a barrel of flour a year. The cost for railroad service in a loaf of bread was half a cent a pound. One day's work by a laborer paid the railroad charges on a year's subsistence. This achievement resulted from the labors of "those called monopolists, Tom Scott, the Garretts, and Vanderbilts."

Atkinson summed it up: "Cornelius Vanderbilt was the greatest and most useful communist of his day, and I mean by that he may be taken as the exponent of a small class of men who have achieved enormous fortunes in a single life, and yet have done more than any other men to bring an ample subsistence within the easy reach

[29] Rockefeller, *op. cit.*, pp. 141–142, 152, 159–160; Phelps, *op. cit.*, pp. 528–529.

of all at a less and less cost, whether cost be measured in labor, in price, in wages, or in purchasing power of the laborer." [30] "Can the anarchist, the communist, the socialist, the protectionist, the free trader, the co-operator, the paper-money man, the knight of labor, the eight-hour man, or the sentimentalist invent or suggest any other method of changing the direction of the industry of the whole community, which would on the whole be so effective in improving the conditions of all, as one which would save five cents a day on food and fuel, the money saved to be devoted to providing better houses in which people may live?" [31] The final justification for the big businessman and big business enterprise was that they lowered prices for the "masses." [32] All in all, as Carnegie concluded, "It will be a great mistake for the community to shoot the millionaires, for they are the bees that make the most honey, and contribute most to the hive even after they have gorged themselves full. . . . Under our present conditions the

[30] *Report of the Committee* [on Education and Labor] *of the Senate* . . . *1885*, III, 343–350; Edward Atkinson, "The Food Question in America and Europe," *Century Magazine*, XXXIII (Dec., 1886), 238–241; Andrew Carnegie, "Wealth and Its Uses," *The Empire of Business* (New York: Doubleday, Page & Co., 1902), p. 132; Perkins, Memo, Oct., 1888, Perkins Private Letters and Memos, R.C.O.

[31] Edward Atkinson, "Remedies for Social Ills," *Forum*, VII (April, 1889), 157.

[32] Rockefeller, *op. cit.*, pp. 158–159; S. C. T. Dodd, "Ten Years of the Standard Oil Trust," *Forum*, XIII (May, 1892), 308–310; Perkins to W. B. Allison, April 9, 1890, Perkins Private Letters and Memos, R.C.O.

millionaire who toils on is the cheapest article which the community secures at the price it pays for him, namely, his shelter, clothing, and food." [33]

This picture of the millionaire as constituting one of an ascetic order toiling in the public service borders on the laughable. It had its sober truth however. Most millionaires and other capitalists did toil and toil hard. Aside from direct statements of allegiance to work, the common attitude was revealed in the attitude of the larger share of the business community toward speculation. Admittedly this was hard to define, for the line between gambling and chance-taking wavered. Rockefeller believed speculation was bad for the speculator, since he got something for nothing; besides the speculator usually lost. Carnegie likewise thought "gamesters die poor." Speculation diverted the businessman's attention from "legitimate business," "producing or dealing in an article which man requires." "The true gold mine" lies in the factory.[34] All this condemnation of chance was in accord with the business spirit of the day—the craving for certainty, the introduction of calculation. The horsemen of disorder and Wall Street, like Fisk, Gould, and Bet-a-Million Gates, did not enjoy a good repute with sober businessmen. When Perkins wrote that "it is a great mistake to suppose that a

---

[33] "Wealth and Its Uses," pp. 138–140.

[34] Rockefeller, *op. cit.*, pp. 152–153; Andrew Carnegie, "The Road to Business Success," *The Empire of Business*, pp. 6–8, 16; Andrew Carnegie, *Autobiography of Andrew Carnegie* (Boston: Houghton, 1920), pp. 176–177.

combination run by a government is better than a combination controlled by Gould," [35] he was trying to show how infinitely bad was the intervention of government in business affairs.

Proud to wear the title "producer," which had taken on the lustre formerly inherent in the word "merchant," the business community was highly dubious of the value of interruptions to the working process. This was true in the case of others, particularly employees. Charles Scaife, owner and manager of the Scaife plant in Pittsburgh, as late as the first decade of this century refused to close the works on Labor Day; his diary entries characterized the day as a "humbug" and a producer of drunks, "harvest for saloon keepers." [36] But employers were just as hard with themselves and with fellow executives. Writing in the mid-eighties a memo on vacations, Perkins laid down as a postulate that certain officers "are employed to attend to the business of the

[35] Lewis Corey, *The House of Morgan* (New York: H. Howard Watt, 1930), pp. 250–251, 288; Perkins to T. M. Marquett, Jan. 3, 1891, Perkins Private Letters and Memos, R.C.O.; *Commercial and Financial Chronicle*, XXIII (Nov. 18, 1876), 487; T. C. Cochran, *Railroad Leaders, 1845–1890: The Business Mind in Action* (Cambridge: Harvard University Press, 1953), pp. 123–124, 214. But see E. L. Godkin, "Commercial Immorality and Political Corruption," *North American Review*, CVII (July, 1868), 250; and *Commercial and Financial Chronicle*, XXII (Feb. 26, 1876), 197–198.

[36] Will and Maxine Schoyer, *Scaife Company and the Scaife Family, 1802–1952* (Pittsburgh: Davis & Warde, 1952), p. 139; *Report of the Committee* [on Education and Labor] *of the Senate . . . 1885*, I, 997.

Railroad Company; and they are expected to do so every day in the year, if necessary." [37] Eventually, since this was the age of calculators, one of these kill-joys discovered, what with Sundays and Saturday half-holidays, that the "subtraction . . . from our real working time" was eighty-five days a year. "It is possible that business and the more serious needs of the community can stand all this," but it was doubtful.[38]

When occasional interruptions to work were thus found insupportable and dangerous, it was natural that the greatest disfavor would be shown to prolonged idleness. To attach a deserved opprobrium to the non-producer, the traditional epithet "drone" was inadequate, except for Carnegie.[39] The era found a better word: the idle person was a "dude." It was hard to define "this new specimen of the genus homo." [40] One educator finally described him as "that creature, harmless and useless, but fair to look upon, called the dude." [41] So great a menace was he that the president of the Throop Polytechnic Institute felt that a girl who had

[37] Memo on Vacations, Jan. 30, 1886, Perkins Private Letters and Memos, R.C.O.

[38] Joel Benton, "The Holiday Hallucination," *North American Review*, CXLVI (April, 1888), 472–473.

[39] *Triumphant Democracy*, pp. 109, 116–118.

[40] *Report of the Committee* [on Education and Labor] *of the Senate . . . 1885*, II, 1204.

[41] A. S. Osborne, "The Disciplinary Value of the Business Course of Study," *N.E.A. Proceedings, 1894* (St. Paul: National Educational Association, 1895), p. 736.

training in domestic science would not grow up to be "the mother whose sons are naturally dudes," [42] and another lesser critic condemned New York City because it raised "nothing but gin-mill statesmen, dudes, and other criminals." [43] Certainly the masters of capital, with the exception of Carnegie, applied themselves to work remorselessly. The executive had his lunch sent in to his place of business and carried his unfinished work home or on vacation.[44] The House of Morgan gained a reputation as a man-killer, and by 1900 all the partners who had aided Morgan to greatness were dead, many of them at premature ages.[45] From Stephen Girard, who said, "When death comes for me, he will find me busy," [46] to Charles C. Scaife, who confided to his diary in 1876, "I cannot be idle; to me, idleness is the most terrible punishment," [47] diligence in business was characteristic and excessive. I recall the wife of one of these workers, although unfortunately I cannot document the allusion, coining an aphorism in parody of a

[42] C. H. Keyes, "The Modifications of Secondary School Courses Most Demanded by the Conditions of Today and Most Ignored by the Committee of Ten," *N.E.A. Proceedings, 1895* (St. Paul: National Educational Association, 1895), p. 736.

[43] *Report of the Committee* [on Education and Labor] *of the Senate . . . 1885*, II, 201.

[44] A. R. Burr, *The Portrait of a Banker: James Stillman, 1850–1918* (New York: Duffield, 1927), p. 96; Cochran, *op. cit.*, p. 216; Carnegie, *Triumphant Democracy*, pp. 117–118.

[45] Corey, *op. cit.*, pp. 253–254.   [46] Diamond, *op. cit.*, p. 12.

[47] Schoyer and Schoyer, *op. cit.*, p. 101; Bliss Perry, *Life and Letters of Henry Lee Higginson* (Boston: Atlantic Monthly Press, 1921), p. 431.

current slogan against women's rights: "Man's place is in the office."

The sanctions for the gospel of work were formidable. "We must labor. It is the divine law: 'In the sweat of thy face shalt thou eat bread until thou return to the ground.' It is the sound economic law. Man must work." [48] Those who obeyed these injunctions were the majority. But, in spite of their example, it proved to be impossible to plug the dike against the dudes. In 1892, E. L. Godkin, editor of the *Nation*, indited an article, "Idleness and Immorality." He detected in America a class which drew its income from stocks and bonds and which was thus able to lead lives of "absolute leisure, of abstaining, that is to say, from all distasteful labor, from doing things they do not like to do." Bored and restless, they travel and indulge in "the distraction of love-making under more or less illicit conditions." Godkin believed that this leisure class should go in for shaping public opinion in desirable directions instead of "polo and tennis and flirtations." [49] Joseph Wharton had thought politics a good field for the "idle rich." Ironically enough, Carnegie was unwilling to rely upon divine or economic law to bring about a reformation. He enthusiastically saluted inheritance taxes or death duties as high as 50 per cent upon the millionaire's estate. Such levies would insure the proper bringing up of chil-

[48] *Report of the Committee* [on Education and Labor] *of the Senate . . . 1885,* I, 983; Perkins to H. L. Higginson, March 8, 1900, Perkins Private Letters and Memos, R.C.O.

[49] *Forum*, XIII (May, 1892), 337–343.

dren of the rich and compel obedience to the Gospel of Wealth.[50]

One way to deal with the motives driving businessmen to work is in terms of generalizations drawn from psychology and sociology: the will to power, desire for recognition and prestige, and other aspects of the craving for assertion or security. The deductive method produces such findings. The reiterated emphasis by Perkins and the *Nation* upon the necessity of profits and upon the acquisition and enjoyment of property were abstractions of the same order derived in much the same way.[51] Concrete statements of their own motives by businessmen are rare: perhaps they felt an examination of this matter was visionary. At least this was true at the beginning of their busineess careers. James E. Caldwell recalled: "As a younger man, I was urged on by the necessity for food and raiment." Later in building a telephone system he was "highly entertained," and in commerce he felt he was engaged in a "fascinating game." [52] This variety of motives resembled to an extraordinary degree that revealed by Joseph E. Sheffield, Connecticut merchant, railroad builder and investor, and donor to Yale. With somewhat more sophistication and at greater length, Sheffield said that as a young man " 'getting gain' was a leading purpose" but he also desired "to *stand well* with my fellows and the

[50] "Wealth," pp. 658–666.

[51] Perkins to T. M. Marquett, Jan. 3, 1891, Perkins Private Letters and Memos, R.C.O.; *Nation*, XXXII (April 14, 1881), 254–255.

[52] *Recollections of a Life Time* (Nashville, Tenn.: Baird-Ward, 1923), p. 244.

people." When he entered commerce, his "mind was called to a higher plane and tone." Of course he expected "to make money. But I distinctly recollect that my *pride of opinion* and great desire to be found *correct* in my *estimates* and *statistics* was paramount to all other considerations." When he became the railroad capitalist of New Haven "*unselfish* public spirit and enterprise" were his leading feelings, "far more intense than any hope of making money." He went into these projects

determined to succeed, and have my reward . . . in the pleasure I sh^d. feel that I, a poor uneducated boy from the village of Millriver (Port Fairfield) should have been instrumental in originating and successfully completing, an enterprise which my country and especially my fellow citizens would appreciate and my children look back to with pride.[53]

In the case of Carnegie, his celebrated definition of the businessman as one who "plunges into and tosses upon the waves of human affairs without a life-preserver in the shape of salary; he risks all," [54] reveals an obsessive, hair-on-the-chest search for total individual independence as motivation.

After all the motives of millionaires did not matter in judging their contribution. In Caldwell's creed "selfish, huckstering trade was the meliorator of the world, because it unites nations in common interests" and "men are seldom so innocently employed as when actively

[53] Retrospective, March, 1876, Sheffield Papers, Yale University Library, quoted in E. C. Kirkland, *Men, Cities and Transportation: A Study in New England History, 1820–1900* (Cambridge: Harvard University Press, 1948), II, 450–451.

[54] "Business," *Empire of Business,* pp. 189–190.

engaged in business." [55] Charles Elliott Perkins was both more searching and more impatient: "Are not the great benefactors of mankind the men who organize industry and help to cheapen the necessaries and conveniences of life? Their motives may be selfish . . . but are they not benefactors all the same?" [56]

Nonetheless I suspect Amercian businessmen were made uneasy by the charge they were "money-mad" and uncomfortable by the assertion that the contributions they made to American life were "materialistic." This was not because it seemed to them ludicrous to

> Hang youah highest hope
> On the pwice, pe'haps of soap [57]

as Edmund Vance Cooke mocked in his excessively nonchalant verse "Fin de Siecle," but because materialism was not spiritual, it was not among the finer things of life. Of the business spokesmen who addressed themselves to this issue,[58] Charles Elliott Perkins was the most trenchant.

Have not great merchants, great manufacturers, great inventors, done more for the world than preachers and

[55] *Op. cit.*, p. 243.

[56] Memo, Oct., 1888, Perkins Private Letters and Memos, R.C.O.

[57] Quoted in Mark Sullivan, *Our Times: The United States, 1900–1925* (New York: Scribner, 1926), I, 289 n.

[58] *Report of the Committee* [on Education and Labor] *of the Senate . . . 1885*, III, 606; Edward Atkinson, "What Shall Be Taxed? What Shall Be Exempt?" *The Industrial Progress of the Nation: Consumption Limited, Production Unlimited* (New York: Putnam, 1890), pp. 267–269; *Nation*, XVI (May 1, 1873), 296.

philanthropists? . . . Can there be any doubt that cheapening the cost of necessaries and conveniences of life is the most powerful agent of civilization and progress? Does not the fact that well-fed and well-warmed men make better citizens, other things being equal, than those who are cold and hungry, answer the question? Poverty is the cause of most of the crime and misery in the world—cheapening the cost of the necessaries and conveniences of life is lessening poverty, and there is no other way to lessen it, absolutely none. History and experience demonstrate that as wealth has accumulated and things have cheapened, men have improved . . . in their habits of thought, their sympathy for others, their ideas of justice as well as of mercy. . . . Material progress must come first and . . . upon it is founded all other progress. . . .[59]

"The true gospel is to enable men to acquire the comforts and conveniences of life by their own efforts, and then they will be wise and good." [60] Alas, that this benign historical process should have any flaw. But "the accumulation of wealth raises the standard of education, and makes it more general; and more general and higher education elevates the standard of morality. It may also be responsible for the political tramp, the non-producer, and some of the modern theorists." [61]

In 1900, Professor Oscar Lovell Triggs of the English Department of the University of Chicago, one of those

[59] Memo, Oct., 1888, Perkins Private Letters and Memos, R.C.O.
[60] Perkins, Memo, July, 1890, Perkins Private Letters and Memos, R.C.O.
[61] Perkins, Memo, Jan. 26, 1885, Perkins Private Letters and Memos, R.C.O.

professorial exhibitionists who likes to startle his students or hearers into listening to him, compared Shakespeare and Rockefeller in their values for humanity and found the latter superior. As he may have expected, he unloosed a flood of comment in the press and elsewhere. "One club sent me a copy of its proceedings in which I saw myself denounced as a silly, conceited ninny—and that by a unanimous vote of the members." [62] Among those who wrote to comfort and congratulate the professor was Perkins, who had once been asked whether Shakespeare or Marshall Field had done more for the world.

I said they couldn't be compared but that, given a suffering world, just starting, there was no doubt that men like Field, who lessen the cost of living, would be of more value than men like Shakespeare, because people suffering from cold and hunger could not possibly get any good from the poets and could only be ready for Shakespeare after Field and Company had warmed and fed them. The *Tribune* says Shakespeare goes on forever while Rockefeller is soon forgotten. The influence of the things Rockefeller does goes on forever also. The world wants both of course. But Rockefeller is much more a necessity than Shakespeare.[63]

"The old nations of the earth creep on at a snail's pace," began Carnegie's *Triumphant Democracy*,

[62] Chicago *Times-Herald*, Oct. 17, 1900. Prof. R. J. Storr, of the University of Chicago, located this item for me.
[63] Letter to O. L. Triggs, Oct. 18, 1900, Perkins Private Letters and Memos, R.C.O.

the Republic thunders past with the rush of the express. The United States, the growth of a single century, has already reached the foremost rank among nations, and is destined soon to outdistance all others in the race. In population, in wealth, in annual savings, and in public credit; in freedom from debt, in agriculture, and in manufactures, America already leads the civilized world.[64]

Historical studies agree with the steel master; these were measurable items for which the census could provide statistical tables. That the energy, ability, and thought of the business community from 1860 to 1900 were an immediate and important reason for this achievement few would deny, although contemporaries sought alternate explanations in the contributions of labor and, more importantly, in "the growth of the country." In any case this question is one also for which historical investigation could presumably find an acceptable answer. Questions on the relative worth of material *versus* another sort of achievement or on the possibility of reaching the same material level by other methods or under other systems, perhaps involving fewer sacrifices and losses—for there were sacrifices and losses—this professor, perhaps "half-baked," prefers to leave to "the volunteer philanthropists" and the "Lady Millionaires." For an answer to such queries we have or can have little or no historical data: we have only the dream and thought of historians.

[64] Page 1.

The Messenger Lectures

IN ITS original form this book consisted of six lectures delivered at Cornell University in April 1956, namely, the Messenger Lectures on the Evolution of Civilization. That series was founded and its title prescribed by Hiram J. Messenger, B.Litt., Ph.D., of Hartford, Connecticut, who directed in his will that a portion of his estate be given to Cornell University and used to provide annually a "course or courses of lectures on the evolution of civilization, for the special purpose of raising the moral standard of our political, business, and social life." The lectureship was established in 1923.

Index

Index

Index